ON IMITATION
AND OTHER ESSAYS

The Library of Liberal Arts
OSKAR PIEST, FOUNDER

The Library of Liberal Arts

ON IMITATION
AND
OTHER ESSAYS

Johann Elias Schlegel

Translated, with an Introduction, by
EDWARD ALLEN McCORMICK
Professor of German, Dartmouth College

The Library of Liberal Arts
published by
THE BOBBS-MERRILL COMPANY, INC.
A Subsidiary of Howard W. Sams & Co., Inc.
Publishers • Indianapolis • New York • Kansas City

Johann Elias Schlegel: 1719-1749
. . . .

809.933
S339o

COPYRIGHT © 1965
THE BOBBS-MERRILL COMPANY, INC.
Printed in the United States of America
Library of Congress Catalog Card Number 64-66075
First Printing

CONTENTS

Translator's Introduction   vii

Selected Bibliography   xxvii

Note on the Text   xxviii

ON IMITATION AND OTHER ESSAYS

On Imitation   3

    I. On Imitation in General   3

    II. On the Nature and Rules of Imitation Insofar as Its Primary Aim Is Pleasure   24

Letter to N. N. Concerning Verse Comedy   51

Translator's Preface to *Le Glorieux*   71

Introduction

The mimetic theory of art, that is, the belief that art is an imitation of nature, is precisely as old as the history of criticism itself. In attempting to answer the basic question in aesthetics—what is art and how is it to be appreciated?—both Plato and Aristotle, the first to enunciate a doctrine and hence to engage in literary speculation,[1] saw art as the attempt to copy reality. Despite certain modifications of their theory, poetry as imitation formed the basis of aesthetic speculation until about the middle of the eighteenth century. The Renaissance writers Boileau, Sidney, Dryden, Pope, Dubos, and, in Germany, Gottsched and Schlegel—all hold more or less firmly to the critical premise that art must imitate nature.

But, if the authority of classical antiquity remained in its essentials unquestioned, the attempts at describing and defining poetry as mimesis from classicism to neoclassicism reveal both variety and continuity. To arrive at a fair assessment of Johann Elias Schlegel in his role as mediator between traditional and modern criticism, we may briefly summarize some of the major statements and restatements of the principle of imitation (as the essential element of poetry) before Schlegel.

Plato believed that poetry was twice removed from the truth. In Book X of the *Republic,* he contrasts the imitator as a maker of images with the maker of realities and finds that the former imitates not what is but what appears to be. He concludes that the imitative art, which expressly extends to poetry, "is an inferior who marries an inferior and has inferior

[1] It would be more accurate to say that, although no Greek developed a doctrine of mimesis prior to Plato and Aristotle, the concept of imitation as the appearance of reality (that is, not the objects of real life themselves) was an accepted part of current critical thought.

offspring." And he adds a final stricture: Not only is the poet twice removed from the truth,[2] but he has no real knowledge of the nature of what he imitates. Had he this knowledge, it is suggested, he would abandon imitation altogether.

As Plato uses the term, "imitation" is not sufficiently defined or limited to a specific activity. It was the achievement of his pupil Aristotle to restrict the word definitely to a single, literal meaning.[3] In at least two places,[4] Aristotle states that art imitates nature. "Imitation" he defines as a man-made presentation of something or some aspect of a thing in a medium other than its natural matter. But the imitator is no mere copyist; "the maker of likenesses," he tells us in the *Poetics*,[5] "must necessarily in all instances represent things in one or other of three aspects, either as they were or are, or as they are said to be or to have been, or as they ought to be." Thus, it must be said that, although art imitates nature, it may do so in a creative sense, for the ideal imitation must surpass the reality.

Aristotle does not offer us a fully developed theory of poetry or a reasonably systematic aesthetic. His principal aim appears to have been to answer Plato's assertion that art was no more than an imitation of an imitation.[6] Yet, however incomplete

---

[2] In a widely quoted passage from the *Republic*, Book X, Socrates and Glaucon are discussing imitation. Using beds as his example, Socrates points out that one may conceive of the existence of no fewer than three beds: one existing in nature and made by God, another that is the work of the carpenter, and a third the work of the painter. Because there can be only one natural author or maker of the bed, however, the carpenter's construction is but an imitation of the real (ideal) bed, and the painter's work an imitation of that which the others make.

[3] Richard McKeon, "Literary Criticism and the Concept of Imitation in Antiquity," *Modern Philology*, XXXIV (August 1936), p. 16.

[4] *Physics* II. 2; *Meteorology* IV. 3.

[5] Chap. 25.

[6] See David Daiches, *Critical Approaches to Literature* (Englewood Cliffs, N. J.: Prentice-Hall, 1956), p. 39: "He is not content with answering Plato's contention that art is but an imitation of an imitation, three removes from the truth; he wishes also to answer specifically Plato's notion that art corrupts by nourishing the passions."

his poetic theory may be, it nonetheless effected the rescue of the artist, opened the way for expression, i.e., the creative aspect, in art, where before there had been the unmistakable suggestion of mere mimicry, and established this liberal concept of imitation as the critical basis for the entire classical tradition.

Two other writers of classical antiquity made significant contributions to the mimesis theory. The first, Horace, introduced the second principal meaning of imitation to critical theory. In his *Epistola ad pisones* ("Art of Poetry"), he advises the would-be writer to select the proper theme. To do this, he must "study the Greek masterpieces: thumb them day and night." And, though he tells the clever imitator to "look to life and morals for his real model," he is quick to add that it was the Greeks "that the Muse endowed with quick wit and rounded utterance."

Although Horace's sophisticated little essay never really confronts the major problems of poetry, its keen awareness of classical models—stick to tradition, he urges, or see that your inventions be consistent—introduces a significant shift from Aristotelian imitation of nature to imitation of art. And such a shift anticipates a central concern of neoclassical criticism.

The final classical theorist to deserve mention is the Roman scholar Longinus, of the third century after Christ.[7] His treatise *On Great Writing* (more frequently called *On the Sublime*) is in the form of a letter to a former fellow student. After describing elevation of style (*hypsos*), Longinus lists the five sources most productive of great writing: vigor of mental conception, strong and inspired emotion, the adequate fashioning of figures (both of speech and of thought), nobility of diction, and dignified and distinguished word arrangement.[8] The first

[7] G. M. A. Grube summarizes the arguments for assigning Longinus' treatise to the first century and finds none of them very convincing. He concludes that "it was either written by Cassius Longinus . . . or by someone else we know nothing about." Longinus, *On Great Writing*, trans. G. M. A. Grube, "The Library of Liberal Arts," No. 79 (New York: The Liberal Arts Press, 1957), p. xx.

[8] *Ibid.*, p. 10.

two, Longinus says, are innate; the others can be attained through the technique of rhetoric. But the order is significant in that it reflects the major concern of *On Great Writing*, namely, poetic genius, a natural gift, rather than acquired learning. Still—and this is the important thing—they cannot be neatly separated. "Nature supplies the first main underlying elements in all cases, but study enables one to define the right amount and appropriate measure on each occasion, and also provides steady training and practice." [9]

It is impossible to determine whether "nature" here applies to the poet, to the poem, or to both in equal measure. Because natural talent "is not usually random or altogether devoid of method," it must be assumed that Longinus had the poet foremost in mind. Yet it is to literary works directly that he turns; indeed, his respect for great models of the past is so high that he claims, with reference to Plato, that one road to greatness is "the emulation and imitation of the great prose writers and poets of the past" [10]—emulation in the sense of following their ways of thinking and feeling (the first two Longinian fountains of eloquence), and imitation in the Horatian sense of following the classics.

In terms of literary theory and, more specifically, the theory of imitation, the centuries between Aristotle and Aristotle *redivivus* must be regarded as a time of relative indifference. Modern scholarship is, of course, unwilling to join Renaissance critics in their reference to the middle ages as barbaric or semibarbaric, yet the fact remains that serious literary and aesthetic speculation was revived only with the reintroduction of Aristotle's *Poetics* in the sixteenth century.[11] A series

[9] *Ibid.*, p. 5.
[10] *Ibid.*, p. 22.
[11] The Middle Ages contributed relatively little to aesthetic speculation, particularly in matters of literary theory. Poetry altogether, it may be said, was held in suspicion insofar as it did not serve as handmaiden to philosophy or theology. J. E. Spingarn offers a concise and useful sum-

of commentaries, editions, and translations of the *Poetics*—beginning with Valla's Latin translation in 1498 and culminating in the extensive commentary by Francesco Robortello in 1548—succeeded in familiarizing Europe with Aristotle. And this meant, in effect, the revival in aesthetics and criticism of the theory of imitation.

However, rediscovery and revival were to remain the major achievements of the Renaissance critics. Relying at first almost exclusively on Aristotle's *Poetics* and Plato's *Republic*, they accepted the classical view of imitation to such an extent that other philosophic bases for poetry were scarcely explored. But, if the major critics of the age—Robortello, Varchi, Castelvetro, Vida, Speroni, Minturno—pay homage to Aristotelian mimesis, they were not unmindful of the Horatian version of imitation. For example, Marco Girolamo Vida, in his *De arte poetica* (1527), pays lip service to the traditional insistence on poetry as an imitation of nature:

> Be sure from Nature never to depart;
> To copy Nature is the task of art.[12]

But he makes it apparent that the study of nature is the study of mankind. His overwhelming concern throughout his treatise is to imitate the "glorious ancients," that is to say, classical writers, for

> The noblest poets own her sovereign sway,
> And ever follow where she leads the way.[13]

The shift from imitation of nature to imitation of art is by no means true of Vida alone. Much of sixteenth-century criticism shows the same deference to the classical dictum that the best poetic models be imitated. Beginning with Guarino's

---

mary of medieval conceptions of poetry in his work, *Literary Criticism of the Renaissance* (2nd ed.; New York: Columbia University Press, 1908), p. 367.

[12] *De arte poetica* II. 455 f., trans. Pitt in Albert S. Clark (ed.), *The Art of Poetry* [of Horace, Vida, Boileau] (Boston, 1892).

[13] *Ibid.*, 456 f.

commentary on the *Art of Poetry* in 1510, Horace was frequently read and interpreted, and by the middle of the century analysis of Horace was regularly combined with the study of Aristotle.

Although Renaissance literary criticism began in Italy, it was not confined to that country. In France, where critical activity is generally held to date from Pelletier's version of Horace's *Art of Poetry* in 1545,[14] the doctrines laid down by the Italians were taken up and restated, sometimes with admirable clarity.

One figure in particular deserves mention—Joachim du Bellay, whose *Deffence et illustration de la langue françoise* ("Defense and Illustration of the French Language," 1549) represents the heart of sixteenth-century French criticism. Drawing heavily on Italian critics, especially Dante, Speroni, and Vida, du Bellay defines imitation as emulation, that is to say, not stealing (as Vida would have it), but the attempt to rival classical beauty. From Aristotle he takes the idea that nature is the object of imitation. But nature is not to be merely copied; it is to be interpreted. Thus, the attitude of man to and in nature becomes more important than the mere presentation or revelation of nature. Du Bellay may be said, then, to represent French Renaissance criticism in rejecting the Platonic notion of imitation as the copy of a copy.

In England, too, one figure may be cited as representative of sixteenth century poetics. Sir Philip Sidney's *Apologie for Poetrie* (written before 1585 but first published in 1595 in two editions, the other bearing the title *Defense of Poesy*) was directly influenced by the Italian critics and was itself responsible for the influence of Aristotelianism in England.

Sidney's definition of poetry offers a combination of the Aristotelian view with Horace's dictum that the poet's aim is "either to profit or to please." "Poesie therefore is an arte of imitation, for so Aristotle termeth it in his word Mimesis, that

---

[14] Cf. Spingarn, p. 171.

TRANSLATOR'S INTRODUCTION

is to say, a representing, counterfetting, or figuring foorth." [15] As to the question of what poetry imitates, Sidney is at once Aristotelian and charmingly vague in the manner of the English gentleman critic of the age: "That imitation whereof Poetry is, hath the most conveniency to Nature of all other, in somuch, that as Aristotle sayeth, those things which in themselves are horrible, as cruell battailes, unnaturall Monsters, are made in poeticall imitation delightfull." [16] His literary examples make it clear, however, that there are many classical writers worthy of emulation. Even more important is his assertion that imagination is superior to fact. Nature's world, says Sidney, "is brasen, the Poets only deliver a golden." [17]

Germany's role in Renaissance critical theory, particularly where imitation is concerned, is negligible. Central to German theory until well into the baroque period were the primacy of the ancients and the full acceptance of *ars, usus, et imitatio,* as established by Celtes' *Ars versificandi* in 1486. The theme of virtually all sixteenth-century German poetics is technique, the learning of forms and rules as a guarantee to artistic achievement. Art is an imitation of nature, and the good poet is thus one who imitates properly. Here, too, the influence of Italy is apparent; classical antiquity is the model on which poets should be guided. Plato and Horace (and sometimes Ovid) are frequently cited, and obedience to the schoolmasterly theoreticians is demanded.

The substitution of reason for imagination, rules for inspiration, that is so common to sixteenth-century German poetic theory also characterizes much of seventeenth-century European criticism. This century also saw the gradual transference of authority in aesthetic matters from Italy to France, where one critic in particular, Boileau, may be credited with carrying the neoclassical ideal of art and nature to ultimate per-

[15] Quoted from Edward Arber's edition ("English Reprints"; London, 1868), p. 26.
[16] *Ibid.*, p. 41.
[17] *Ibid.*, p. 25.

fection. Boileau's *L'Art poétique* ("Art of Poetry," 1674), although it did not greatly influence French poetry, embodies most of the important aspects of seventeenth-century French criticism. His statements on imitation may be taken also as representative of the prevailing attitude.

> You, then, that would the comic laurels wear,
> To study nature be your only care.[18]

These lines are strongly reminiscent of Vida, as altogether the major part of his *Art of Poetry* resembles a patchwork quilt whose pieces remind one first of Horace, then of Vida and other Renaissance critics, and finally of Aristotle. In the first canto, Boileau tells the poet to use reason—"always let sense accompany your rime"—which of course represents something new; but, on the whole, his advice is still the same as that of his predecessors. The poet is to imitate nature. To be certain that he does it correctly, he is to turn to the ancients and imitate them.

In England, Dryden's *Essay of Dramatic Poesie,* published in 1668, continues the plea for imitation of the ancients, who have been "faithful imitators and wise observers of that Nature which is so torn and ill represented in our plays." The poet, says Dryden, must imitate well,

> for a play is still an imitation of Nature; we know we are to be deceived, and we desire to be so; but no man ever was deceived but with a probability of truth. . . . since the mind of man does naturally tend to truth; and therefore the nearer anything comes to the imitation of it, the more it pleases.[19]

However, in his *Defence of an Essay of Dramatic Poesie* (1668), he no longer insists that an imitation be measured solely by its fidelity to truth. One great reason, he says, "why prose is not to be used in serious plays, is, because it is too near the nature of converse: there may be too great a likeness." [20]

[18] *L'Art poétique* III. 359 f.
[19] *Of Dramatic Poesy and Other Critical Essays,* ed. G. Watson, "Everyman Library," No. 568 (London: Dent & Sons, 1962), I, 79–80.
[20] *Ibid.,* I, 114.

The closing years of the seventeenth century saw a turn to verse criticism, such as we see it in France with Boileau. In 1680, a verse translation of Horace's *Art of Poetry* appeared, and in 1683 Dryden and Soames translated Boileau's *Art of Poetry*. A host of other versified essays followed, and the way was open for Pope's *Essay on Criticism*, published in 1711, which continued the tradition of Horace and Boileau.

German baroque, as the seventeenth century is commonly, if erroneously, called, produced only one critic of note, Martin Opitz. Although a mediocre poet at best, his *Buch von der teutschen Poeterei* ("Book on German Poetry"), written in 1624, stands as the most important and influential poetic statement of the century by a German. Opitz' treatise is a rather loose collection of rules and illustrations borrowed from classical, Italian, and French criticism. His knowledge of Aristotle appears to have been derived from Scaliger and Daniel Heinsius, an early Dutch commentator on the *Poetics*. He seems to have known Horace directly, but it was to Renaissance criticism that he owes most.

Poetry, says Opitz, was originally nothing more than disguised theology. Although the poet is born, not made (he is called the *Poet von Natur*), he must learn the right technique from Greek and Latin works. As to rules, Opitz is careful to cite foreign authorities as "confirmation" of his own beliefs. What these latter were precisely—apart from the conviction that poetry is teachable—is never made clear, and for that reason it is all the more astounding that the "Book on German Poetry" went through no fewer than eleven separate editions in the seventeenth century alone.[21]

At the beginning of the eighteenth century, neoclassicism was firmly established in all the countries under discussion here. Indeed, we have seen that most of the major questions, especially in regard to imitation, had already been asked, if not entirely settled, in the sixteenth century. What the first

[21] Cf. Bruno Markwardt, *Geschichte der deutschen Poetik* (Berlin: Walter De Gruyter & Co., 1956), II, 45.

half of the eighteenth century did was to continue to apply the "natural laws" that were valid for criticism as well as for science. The theory of imitation was restated and applied to literature and the other arts; Aristotle and Horace were constantly cited as the classical authorities in matters of genre; reason and good taste as opposed to excessive enthusiasm continued in their dominant position; and rules, lastly, with an accompanying insistence on formal criteria, remained at the center of neoclassical orthodoxy. Three critics in particular may be cited as representative of the neoclassical view of imitation—Pope, Dubos, and Gottsched.

Pope's *Essay on Criticism* has been called the last of the major critical verse essays in the manner of Horace. The advice given in this essay, which deals directly with laws the critic should follow, is to follow nature:

> First follow nature, and your judgment frame
> By her just standard, which is still the same.[22]

Changing his stance slightly (but predictably), he turns to the ancients—

> Those Rules of old discover'd, not devis'd,
> Are Nature still, but Nature methodiz'd [23]

—and suggests that we no longer have to look at nature. The classics will serve as well:

> Learn hence for ancient rules a just esteem;
> To copy nature is to copy them.[24]

However, when he equates the imitation of Homer with imitation of nature, he is attempting to reconcile two distinct approaches. In Pope's own time, critics were quick to point out that the *Essay on Criticism* was unsuccessful in this, but the point is that he alone undertook to merge fully classical standards and reason, the catchword of the eighteenth century. In this vital respect, he goes beyond Vida and Boileau.

[22] *Essay on Criticism*, 68 f.
[23] *Ibid.*, 88 f.
[24] *Ibid.*, 139 f.

With Dubos' *Réflexions critiques sur la poésie et sur la peinture* ("Critical Reflections on Poetry, Painting, and Music," 1719), aesthetic speculation is rejoined to poetic theory, which had dominated critical thinking since the Renaissance. The constant theme of the *Critical Reflections* is that imitation is but a pale image of nature ("The most finished imitation hath only an artificial existence, or a borrowed life" [25]); and, having admitted this, Dubos goes on to search out its good qualities. The art of imitation, he explains in Chapter 10, is more engaging than the very subject of imitation; the pleasure imitation gives is pure pleasure, and the passions aroused, copies of real passions. Poetry and painting seek to arouse these copied or artificial passions and thereby to afford us aesthetic enjoyment. Painting makes use of natural signs or symbols of expression, whereas poetry uses artificial signs, that is, words. Anticipating Lessing's argument in the *Laocoön*, Dubos explains that painting can represent but a single instant, whereas poetry presents a succession of intants.[26]

It is an irony of history that, under the influence of Dubos (and, to a lesser degree, Bouhours), French rationalism as found in aesthetics and criticism began to lose its force, while Germany, under the literary dictatorship of Gottsched and with a respect for French literature and criticism that approached blind adulation, remained firmly planted on the side of reason and rules. To make the intensity of the emotion aroused in the spectator the main criterion of aesthetic value in art, as Dubos had done, would have been sheer heresy to Gottsched. This was to be the task of the Swiss critics Bodmer and Breitinger, aided by one of Gottsched's own students, Johann Elias Schlegel.

For better or worse, Johann Christoph Gottsched enjoyed

---

[25] *Réflexions critiques* I. 23, in *Critical Reflections on Poetry, Painting, and Music*, trans. Thomas Nugent (London, 1748), II, 23.
[26] Cf. Lessing, *Laocoön*, trans. E. A. McCormick, "The Library of Liberal Arts," No. 78 (New York: The Bobbs-Merrill Company, Inc., 1962), p. 77.

an authority in literary matters during the second quarter of the eighteenth century that was tantamount to absolute law. Some of the causes he espoused and the ideas he expressed were new; others were taken over from the seventeenth century via France; still others were inherited from his baroque predecessor, Martin Opitz. A full statement of Gottsched's critical position may be found in his *Versuch einer critischen Dichtkunst* ("Attempt at a Critical Art of Poetry"), first published in 1729 and later revised several times.[27] The *Critische Dichtkunst*, as it is commonly called, is a compilation of the ideas of various other critics, rather than the product of his own thought. It begins with a translation of Horace's *Art of Poetry* and has as its stated goal "to show that the inner nature of poetry consists in the imitation of nature."

However, since Gottsched himself was not fully clear as to what imitation of nature means, it is not surprising that nowhere in the entire *Critische Dichtkunst* is a precise definition attempted. Nature is sometimes called beautiful, sometimes reasonable or rational (*vernünftig*), and sometimes simply well known (*bekannt*). Occasionally it is made synonymous with "truth." The meaning of "imitation" likewise varies, denoting first a mere copying, then forming or modeling (*bilden*) in a natural manner, and finally outright invention (*erdichten*). It does seem apparent, at least, that Gottsched has in mind the use of nature, as it is known to man and recognized as beautiful, as a model for the work of art. The object of imitation, he seems to be saying, is a combination of three things: nature, truth, and reason.

Gottsched lists five requirements for the poet (whom he calls "a skillful imitator of all natural things"): a strong imagination, great sagacity, excellent intellect, a constant study of things, and a thorough knowledge of man. Typically, he

[27] In the course of the later editions (1737, 1742, and 1751), Gottsched revised and expanded his views on poetry, so that we may refer to the 1751 edition, some eight hundred pages long, as the fullest statement of Gottsched's critical and aesthetic position. This edition was republished in 1962 by the Wissenschaftliche Buchgesellschaft, Darmstadt. Subsequent page references are to this 1751 edition.

warns that the first requirement must constantly be held in check by common sense, that is, healthy reason. Furthermore, he appears to be unaware of the fact that it is the poet's ability to invent, to create what he calls a fable (Gottsched's highest form of imitation!), that raises him above mere copying.[28] By contradicting himself and moving from imitation as a faithful reproduction of reality to a representation of what is possible or probable, he demonstrates, not only his inability to create a consistent theory of poetry, but also the necessity to go beyond strict imitation and admit other equally important concepts, for example, inspiration, invention, and genius. Though he comes precariously close to the realization that art moves away from nature and that its essence lies primarily in its *dis*similarity to nature, he never actually arrived at this critical insight.

With the writings of Johann Elias Schlegel (1719–1749), we reach a point in German critical theory where art as imitation of nature and, more generally, the prescriptive aspects of neoclassicism begin to disintegrate. Schlegel is a more vigorous critic than Gottsched and much more original; but his premise is still very Gottschedian—art is an imitation of nature. His importance lies, rather, in the way that he argues his points and in his willingness to ask and to pursue systematically questions of a most fundamental kind. In this vital respect, he places himself at a considerable remove from Gottsched's neoclassical doctrine and anticipates Germany's assumption of

[28] In Chapter 4, "On the Three Kinds of Poetic Imitation," Gottsched states that imitation of nature can occur in three ways: "The first is a mere description or very lively depiction of a natural subject that one paints clearly for his readers in all of its attributes, beauties or flaws, perfections or imperfections" (p. 142). "Another kind of imitation occurs when the poet himself assumes the role of another person and dictates to him such words, gestures, and actions as would be appropriate for him in certain situations" (p. 144). "Yet even this highly difficult kind of imitation does not constitute the real essence of poetry. It is primarily the fable [an event that might happen in certain circumstances and that contains a useful moral truth] that represents the origin and soul of all poetry" (p. 148).

leadership in philosophical and critical thought under Gotthold Ephraim Lessing.

All of Schlegel's critical and theoretical writings fall in the years from 1739 to 1747. Within that brief span, we may distinguish two separate periods of activity, the first beginning with his *Auszug eines Briefes, welcher einige kritische Anmerkungen über die Trauerspiele der Alten und Neuern enthält* ("Excerpt from a Letter on Ancient and Modern Tragedy"), written during the first months of his stay in Leipzig (1739), and ending with his longest critical essay, the important work *Abhandlung von der Nachahmung* ("On Imitation"), written in 1742. The second period does not begin until almost three years after Schlegel took up his duties in Copenhagen as private secretary to the Saxon minister at the Danish court. This was early in 1743. In 1745, his verse translation of Destouches' *Le Glorieux* ("The Conceited Count") appeared, with the short preface that has been included in the present volume. His last piece of criticism, *Gedanken zur Aufnahme des dänischen Theaters* ("Thoughts on the Improvement of the Danish Theater"), was written in 1747 but not published until seventeen years after his tragically early death in 1749, at the age of thirty.

In addition to the works just mentioned, six others of a critical or theoretical nature were written during those nine years of activity. The "Letter to N.N. Concerning Verse Comedy" was published in 1740 in Gottsched's journal, *Critische Beiträge* ("Critical Contributions").[29] In 1741, Schlegel made three additional contributions to Gottsched's periodical: an essay on Johann Klag's *Herodes* (*Herodes der Kindermörder*), *Democritus, ein Todtengespräche* ("Democritus, Conversations

[29] The full title of the *Critische Beiträge* is *Beyträge zur critischen Historie der deutschen Sprache, Poesie und Beredsamkeit, herausgegeben von einigen Mitgliedern der Deutschen Gesellschaft in Leipzig* (8 vols., Leipzig, 1732–1744). Schlegel's verse comedy essay appeared in Volume III of the *Werke*, ed. Johann Heinrich Schlegel (5 vols.; Copenhagen and Leipzig, 1761–1770), pp. 65–94. It is also printed in Antoniewicz' edition of the aesthetic and dramaturgical writings and in the newest edition of Schlegel's works, edited by Werner Schubert (see below, p. xxviii).

with the Dead"), and *Vergleichung Shakespears und Andreas Gryphs* ("Shakespeare and Andreas Gryphius Compared"). His *Abhandlung, daß die Nachahmung der Sache, der man nachahmet, zuweilen unähnlich werden müsse* ("How Imitation Must Sometimes Be Unlike the Original") was also written in 1741, but not published until 1745, presumably because it opposed so many of Gottsched's current theories. A final essay, *Von der Würde und Majestät des Ausdrucks im Trauerspiele* ("On the Dignity and Majesty of Expression in Tragedy"), appeared in 1747 as a preface to the Copenhagen edition of the dramatic works and was later included in the 1764 edition of Schlegel's collected works under the title given above. A brief essay on the establishment of a national theater in Copenhagen was also printed in 1747, but contains little of relevance or importance to Schlegel's critical theories.

Though it would not be to our purpose to discuss at length here what Schlegel means by imitation and how he attempts to answer the question of art's relation to nature—on these points, the essays may speak for themselves—a few remarks on the background of the selections comprising the present volume should be of help in understanding his imitation theory.

The "Letter to N.N. Concerning Verse Comedy" or, to give it its German title, *Schreiben an den Herrn N.N. über die Komödie in Versen,* was written at a time when Schlegel's interest in verse as a means of dramatic expression was perhaps strongest. The previous year (1740) had seen the first of his verse plays produced at the Leipzig theater; this play, *Die entführte Dose,* ("The Pilfered Snuffbox") was, in Schlegel's words, "a poor piece" (*ein schlechtes Stück*).[30] Two other comedies were written during the Leipzig stay and another begun but left unfinished. Unfortunately, too little remains of these comedies—we have only a few scenes from the *Snuffbox* and scattered notes on another play. The third, *Der geschäfftige Müssiggänger,* ("The Busy Idler"), written in 1742, is in prose— to enable us to form a clear notion of the relationship between poetic theory and practice. But it may be said that Schlegel's

[30] *Werke,* ed. Schlegel, II, 621.

interest in questions of theory was probably greater during these last years at Leipzig.

The immediate occasion for writing the essay on verse comedy was Gottlob Benjamin Straube's *Versuch eines Beweises, daß eine gereimte Comödie nicht gut seyn könne* ("Attempt to Prove That a Rhymed Comedy Cannot Be Good"), which appeared in Number 23 of the *Critical Contributions*. Straube, a pupil of Gottsched, was certain of his mentor's approval, for Gottsched had pleaded for the abolition of "annoying rhyming" in tragedies and "theater poems" in an essay written as early as 1732. Though he was later to modify this view considerably, it was as good as law in 1740, when Straube undertook his awkward attack on rhyme. "Can anything be closer to nature," he asks, "than the person who is himself nature? And must not the constant consonance of rhyme cry out against nature?" [31]

Schlegel's reply, which he disguises as a letter and in which he refers to "certain gentlemen" (Straube and Gottsched), offers a defense, not only of verse comedy, but of poetic form generally. His main source was presumably (absolute certainty is out of the question in view of Schlegel's general reluctance to cite sources of any kind) a seventeenth-century French scholar, the Abbé Fraguier. Beyond the narrower question of rhymed verse for comedy, Schlegel's essay lays the groundwork for a later and more systematic examination of imitation. Three assertions in particular represent significantly new advances over Gottsched. The ultimate purpose of imitation is no longer didactic or moral; it lies, rather, in the pleasure it affords. Because pleasure-provoking qualities are to be found in the treatment of a subject rather than in the subject itself, it may be concluded that pleasure has nothing to do with what is being imitated. According to Schlegel, ugliness, too, can be a fitting subject for imitation. Finally, his defense of verse comedy on grounds that the imitation need not be similar to the original in all respects but may even be dissimilar

[31] *Critische Beiträge*, VI, 467.

to it strikes a breach in his relations with the Gottsched school that is not to be closed again. Schlegel is at pains not to name his opponents and, wherever possible, to subscribe to Gottsched's views, but the deep-seated differences in their concept of imitation as greatest possible fidelity to nature or, on the other hand, as a pleasing similarity based on awareness of deception or illusion made continued association impossible.

The essay "On Imitation" constitutes Schlegel's major contribution to the imitation theory. This work builds on the fundament established by the essay on verse comedy. Instead of a slavish copying of nature, Schlegel recommends a partial (and intentional!) departure from the model. How this is to be accomplished depends on the demands of each work—an example of empirical research and sound inductive procedure that makes Schlegel unique among German aestheticians of the early eighteenth century. The second major advance in aesthetic theory offered by "On Imitation" is also anticipated in the verse-comedy essay: pleasure is the ultimate goal of imitation. However, Schlegel remains deeply indebted in other respects to the traditional view of art as imitation of nature or reality. Like Gottsched, he is convinced that rules can be established to enable one to imitate all the better. Moreover, he sometimes deserts his important insight that art is not really nature and is not intended to be. For example, when he argues (in Section 20) that accusations of unnaturalness on the part of the imitator would disappear if the imitator accommodated himself to his audience's ideas, he is lapsing into a kind of Gottschedian naturalism. Yet the bulk of evidence is on the positive side. Although Schlegel never rejects the principle of art as imitation of nature, he realizes that "the choice of the degree and medium of imitation—as well as the original itself—is entirely open." This is tantamount to saying that the artist need not imitate more closely than he chooses. He must not confuse his audience, to be sure, but he is permitted to move away from nature as long as communication of pleasure is not sacrificed.

Unfortunately, Schlegel's major effort in aesthetics failed to achieve the attention and influence it merited.[32] In 1746, the Abbé Batteux published his famous treatise on *Les beaux arts réduits à un même principe* ("The Fine Arts Reduced to One Principle"). The single principle was, naturally enough, imitation of nature or, more precisely, of beautiful nature. Although Batteux's treatise is decidedly inferior to "On Imitation" in virtually every respect except those of style and elegance, it had the advantage of having been written by a Frenchman at a time when this very fact automatically signified probable superiority. Also, the support given Batteux's unified view of the arts by Diderot and d'Alembert in the *Encyclopédie* made the *Beaux arts* one of the influential works of the eighteenth century. By the time Schlegel's essay appeared in convenient book form—in 1764, just two years before Lessing's *Laocoön*—criticism had moved to a point where, for Germany at least, its imitative premises and the excessively high regard for French drama were no longer incontestable truths.

Schlegel's translation of Philippe (Néricault) Destouches' play *Le Glorieux* appeared in Leipzig in 1745. The "Preface" contributes nothing substantially new to Schlegel's theory of verse comedy or of imitation generally; however, as a summary and reformulation of the case against naturalism (opera, too, is defended in its use of "sung tones," that is, in letting its heroes sing of their deeds and the like), it deserves serious consideration. Of special significance is Schlegel's insistence on impartiality and the fact that he admits having encountered "trouble and difficulties" in translating the play. He goes so far as to grant the detractors of verse comedy their point in

---

[32] This was partly owing to the fact that the essay was published piecemeal. Part I, "On Imitation in General," appeared in 1742 in Number 29 of the *Critische Beiträge;* the first half of Part II appeared in 1743 in Number 31 of the same periodical; the rest of the essay appeared in 1745 in Number 5 of a new journal, *Neuer Büchersaal* ("New Library"), which Gottsched had founded after the demise of the *Critische Beiträge*. See Antoniewicz, pp. xii ff., and Elizabeth M. Wilkinson, *Johann Elias Schlegel: A German Pioneer in Aesthetics* (Oxford: Basil Blackwell, 1945), pp. 277 f.

stressing the difficulty of preserving naturalness in verse dialogue. In regard to theory, he feels himself to be on safe ground; just as marble is the sculptor's medium and paint and canvas are the painter's, so is verse one possible medium open to the poet. When it comes to practice, however, he is ready to admit that, although the French have produced verse plays with natural dialogue, the case for German verse comedy has not yet been made.

It is evident that the "Translator's Preface" and its predecessor, the essay on verse comedy, do not actually justify verse as a poetic medium. Their real meaning and significance go deeper; the case is made for the freedom of the artist to choose his medium. And medium, Schlegel says in his "Preface," is inviolable; if it does not permit close similarity to the original, that is of no grave consequence. There are, he realizes, such limits to imitation as similarity and probability. And this recognition is the key to Schlegel's entire theory of imitation. Art may be an imitation of nature, but, in the very act of imitating, it moves away from reality.[33] We have seen from this brief survey of the imitation theory that Schlegel has made no radical discovery. Yet his writings on imitation constitute not only the outermost limits to which the theory of imitation may be stretched; it is the first reasonably consistent aesthetic system of the German Enlightenment. He alone was able to make mimesis a fruitful concept for the later Enlightenment.

EDWARD ALLEN McCORMICK

Norwich, Vermont
March 1965

---

[33] Wilkinson offers an excellent summary of Schlegel's imitation theory, particularly in its advance over Gottsched. See *ibid.,* pp. 53–64 *et passim.*

Selected Bibliography

DAICHES, DAVID. *Critical Approaches to Literature.* Englewood Cliffs, N.J.: Prentice-Hall, Inc., 1956.

GLUNZ, HANS H. *Die Literarästhetik des europäischen Mittelalters.* Frankfurt-am-Main: Vittorio Klostermann, 1937. 2nd edition, 1963.

HALL, VERNON, JR. *A Short History of Literary Criticism.* New York: New York University Press, 1963.

HATHAWAY, BAXTER. *The Age of Criticism: The Late Renaissance in Italy.* Ithaca, N.Y.: Cornell University Press, 1962.

MCKEON, RICHARD. "Literary Criticism and the Concept of Imitation in Antiquity," *Modern Philology,* XXXIV (August 1936), 1–35.

MARKWARDT, BRUNO. *Geschichte der deutschen Poetik.* Volume II, *Aufklärung, Rokoko, Sturm und Drang.* Berlin: Walter de Gruyter & Co., 1956.

SAINTSBURY, GEORGE. *A History of Criticism and Literary Taste in Europe.* Volume II, *From the Renaissance to the Decline of Eighteenth-Century Orthodoxy.* New York: Dodd, Mead, and Co., 1902.

SMITH, JAMES HARRY, and PARKS, EDD WINFIELD, eds. *The Great Critics.* 3rd edition. New York: Norton & Co., 1951.

SPINGARN, J. E. *Literary Criticism in the Renaissance.* 2nd edition. New York: Columbia University Press, 1962.

WANIEK, GUSTAV. *Gottsched und die deutsche Literatur seiner Zeit.* Leipzig: Breitkopf & Härtel, 1897.

WEINBERG, BERNARD. *A History of Literary Criticism in the Italian Renaissance.* 2 vols. Chicago: University of Chicago Press, 1961.

xxviii ON IMITATION AND OTHER ESSAYS

WELLEK, RENÉ. *A History of Modern Criticism: 1750–1950.* Volume I, *The Later Eighteenth Century.* New Haven, Conn.: Yale University Press, 1955.

WILKINSON, ELIZABETH M. *Johann Elias Schlegel: A German Pioneer in Aesthetics.* Oxford: Basil Blackwell, 1945.

WIMSATT, WILLIAM K., JR., and BROOKS, CLEANTH. *Literary Criticism: A Short History.* New York: Alfred A. Knopf, 1957.

WOLFF, EUGEN. *Johann Elias Schlegel: Eine Monographie.* Berlin, 1889.

Note on the Text

This translation is based on the text of Johann von Antoniewicz' German edition of Schlegel's aesthetic and dramaturgical writings. In those few instances in which a reading seemed ambiguous or otherwise doubtful, I have consulted Werner Schubert's more recent edition of the works, which lists all his variants from the collected works of 1761–1770. Because Schubert consulted Antoniewicz' text as well, it may be assumed that this translation is based on the best reading available.

The full titles of the editions are:

Johann Elias Schlegels Werke. Edited by JOHANN HEINRICH SCHLEGEL. 5 vols. Copenhagen and Leipzig, 1761–1770.

Johann Elias Schlegels aesthetische und dramaturgische Schriften. Edited by JOHANN VON ANTONIEWICZ. "Deutsche Literaturdenkmale des 18. und 19. Jahrhunderts," Volume XXVI. Heilbronn, 1887.

JOHANN ELIAS SCHLEGEL. *Ausgewählte Werke.* Edited by WERNER SCHUBERT. Weimar: Arion Verlag, 1963.

E. A. M.

ON IMITATION
AND OTHER ESSAYS

On Imitation

I. ON IMITATION IN GENERAL

I have long considered a closer examination of the concept of imitation indispensable if, in judging poetry, we are to rely more on established reasons than on our opinion or our "practiced" feeling. We cannot know for certain whether we are justified in calling a thing natural or unnatural, nor can we, in my opinion, determine the limits of probability, until this concept has been explicitly defined. I shall undertake this examination and attempt to prove my points without making my presentation too dry or elegant. But I shall appeal also to the latitude inherent in this method of teaching by neither citing nor refuting what others have maintained about this or that proposition and by being permitted to go my own way without concerning myself with those I chance to meet along the way or with those whose footsteps I shall encounter now and again. Despite the fact that the subject of my treatise forms the basis of many of the arts, upon which the most reliable rules for painting and music rest, I shall for the most part apply the rules to poetry. Still, it will be necessary to refer to the aforementioned arts in order to confirm by experience what is already proven. And if I should occasionally use words in an unaccustomed way, it is a liberty that will readily be tolerated since one must define one's terms and since this cannot be done without a certain freedom of terminology in an area hitherto not broadly treated in such a way.

I shall divide this treatise into two parts. In the first, I shall treat my subject without regard to its ultimate purpose; in the second, however, I shall consider the subject insofar as its ultimate purpose is pleasure. I shall not concern myself with other aspects simply because pleasure is the principal and final object of imitation in the arts.

1. One customarily gives the name "imitation" both to the act of imitating and to the thing that is made to resemble another. The first is done in calling poetry an imitation of nature; the second occurs when the term "imitation" is applied to a composition in which the manner of thinking of another has been closely followed. However, in order to avoid ambiguity, I am obliged to reject the latter use of the term (as well as any others one might find) and to explain that by "imitation" I understand nothing more than *an action, the purpose of which is to produce something similar to another thing.* One will discover by experience that there is no real imitation without the accompanying intent to produce something similar. Not everything similar to another is imitated. A clear example of this is to be seen in the fact that we can never justifiably say that a poet has imitated a passage by someone else unless we are certain that at the time he wrote he did not have the other's work before him. Because I shall frequently find it necessary to refer to an object intentionally made to resemble another and because I cannot in such a case make use of the term *Nachahmung* ["imitation"], I shall call that object an "imitation" or "representation" (*Bild*) and use the terms "original" or "model" (*Vorbild*) to designate that which the imitation is made to resemble.

2. In our explanation of imitation, those terms most deserving of additional clarification must be expounded further so that the concept of imitation will be better able to produce rules by which imitation can be governed. It is especially necessary to explain the term "similarity" in such a way that we may see clearly how pleasure based on imitation arises and more readily understand how to go about imitating things. To this end, a concept employed by teachers of practical geometry seems most appropriate. We shall extend this concept only far enough for it to apply to things other than geometric quantities and their ratios. *A thing whose parts stand in the same relation to one another as that prevailing among the parts of another thing is similar to this latter.* As to the meaning of "relation" (*Verhältnis*), one will be acquainted with this term

from philosophy; *we speak of relation when there is a quality in the one from which a quality in the other can be explained,* or however else one wishes to describe what Latin scholars call by the general name *relatio,* under which all modes of regarding a thing in its relation to another may be grouped.

In our theory of imitation, we are concerned only with things having to do with the imagination. Hence, we can certainly assume the existence of parts in that which we are imitating. Indeed, it is impossible to imitate things without imagining to ourselves parts of those things. If, following the concept of those who have written on metaphysics, we want to say that whatever has the same quality (*Beschaffenheit*) as something else is similar to it, then we must also separate in our minds the qualities from the thing itself and consequently consider whether the parts of those things in question are similar to one another. However, we shall also have to concede that, if the similarity is to make any impression at all, the same relation must exist among the parts of the one as exists among those of the other. For, if they should stand in a different relation to one another, there would be, strictly speaking, no longer precisely those qualities in both, but others instead. So one may choose whatever explanation one will, for the one will say as much as the other. But the one we borrow from the geometricians will have the advantage of offering more to the imagination and consequently of showing us how easily the pleasure arising from similarity may be derived from it.

In illustration of these concepts, I shall take an example from the same source from which I borrowed my explanations. I shall assume that the original has two parts, A and B. In part *a* of the imitation (*Bild*), there will then have to be the same quality as is found in A and from which something in B can be explained. In part *b* of the imitation, the same quality must reside as is in B and which can be explained from A. Furthermore, both qualities in *a* and *b* must be explicable separately in the same way as those in A and B are. This occurs in the same manner as when I have two ratios of relations in mathematics that are equal, e.g., $3:9 = 6:18$. Here,

3 has a quality in common with 6, namely, the fact that they both go three times into the number to which they stand in ratio; and 9 and 18 likewise have the quality in common of being divisible three times by the number to which they stand in ratio. In addition, they must stand in uniform relation to each other. For I could not say $3:9 = 6 \times 18$. This means that they have the same relation, and it shows at the same time a further requirement: They must possess like qualities among their corresponding parts, which can be explained uniformly from one another. One can readily conceive of this relation existing in painting, sculpture, and music, because in these arts the imitation (*Bild*) is external and the relation of the parts of the imitation strikes one's senses, whereas the relation of the parts of the original impresses itself on our imagination, as we have seen this relation before.

I think that, in the case of poetry, however, an explanation is needed. Imitation in poetry can be of two kinds. It can be dramatic, that is to say, it can consist of imitated speech, in which the representation is likewise external and consists of the words that we hear themselves. Only in such a case does our intellect compare the thoughts of poetic speech and their interconnection to the thoughts in the ordinary speech of a person about the character and emotions that poetic speech imitates. All poems in which the poet expresses his own emotions are of this kind. Most odes, too, belong to this group. Or imitation in poetry can be historical, that is, it can narrate or describe. In this case, the imitation (*Bild*) is not external but is awakened in us solely by the words we hear, and we accordingly compare the relation of the parts of the imitation created by these words in our imagination to the thing that is being narrated or described itself or, rather, to the image of the thing in our minds. I shall explain this more fully later. Because we are presently concerned only with similarity, however, I believe that it will suffice to offer a poetic simile as an example of how we can also observe relations or ratios (even though they be of the same kind) in things other than those that can be measured.

> Wie ein gefärbtes Glas, wodurch die Heitre stralt
> Des Auges Urtheil täuscht und sich in allem mahlt:
> So thut das Vorurtheil, es zeigt uns alle Sachen
> Nicht wie sie an sich sind, nein, wie sie es will machen.[1]

Who can fail to see here that a tinted glass is to the eye as prejudice is to understanding, for both deceive and both depict things differently from what they are? The former imparts its color to the rays, whereas the latter lends to everything that enters our soul the sort of tinge that is in harmony with such prejudice. The things that form an image in our mind stand in the same relation to our understanding as do rays to the eye; and, as the rays are to the colored glass, so are the things to an a priori judgment, for they are falsified by it. Everywhere we see only one kind of relation. If we wanted to continue our search, we could find other instances of correspondence.

3. *If things are to be similar to one another, their parts must stand in the same relation. Thus, the parts of the imitation must correspond to the parts of the original, and an imitation is dissimilar to the original and hence faulty if its parts do not have this relation to the original's parts.*

To explain this similarity further, I shall give examples of both material and immaterial things. It is certain that an imitation will not bear much resemblance to any person unless the legs have the same relation to the head as prevails in a normal person (be it that the legs are too short or too long); and it is certain that an arm that has been broken off a statue and replaced in an incorrect manner will cause that statue to be dissimilar to a real person, etc. And it is likewise certain that violations of material subjects can often be found in poems. For example, when Gryphius says,

---

[1] As a colored glass, through which a clear light beams,
deceives the eye and paints itself upon everything:
So does prejudice; it shows us all things
Not as they are in themselves, but
As it wants to make them.

—Albrecht von Haller (1708–1788), Swiss poet-scientist whose poems are characterized by nature description pronouncedly didactic in tone and intent.

> Wie, wenn das schnelle Blut aus vollen Adern dringet
> Und schäumend durch die Luft aus offnen Röhren springet,[2]

he has, to be sure, observed everything that one customarily sees when blood spurts from an open artery: open arteries, the gushing forth of the blood, its rapidity and force, the fact that it spurts up, and its bubbling. All these are components one can observe and isolate in one's mind. But still the poet has committed the error of improperly combining the bubbling of the blood with the other attributes, thus failing to achieve precisely that relation among them that we are accustomed to see in nature. It seems to me that the blood's spume is not in the air, but on the ground, where the blood has spurted. We see, then, that only dissimilarity can result when the parts are not placed in the exact combination that we observe in nature. This is likewise true of immaterial subjects. Suppose we take all the thoughts that occur to a person during a time of agitation and do no more than change their order and sequence. Let us then see whether it is the very same agitation. Agitated emotions are distinguished from a calm consideration of things as often by their combination as by the thoughts themselves. The strength and weakness, as well as the difference of feelings, often arise from nothing more than a different combination and sequence of thoughts. For example, in Opitz' translation of *The Trojan Women,* Andromache is speaking merely in a pleading and humiliated way when, in order to save her son from death, she says:

> Schau ihn doch nur recht an!
> Soll er den Schutt der Stadt zu räumen sich getrauen?
> Soll dieser Hände Kraft ein Troja wieder bauen?

---

2   As when fast-flowing blood surges from full arteries
    And from open tubes spurts foaming through the air.

Andreas Gryphius (1616–1664) was one of the leading representatives of German baroque poetry. In a century not distinguished for its drama, he must also be considered the leading dramatist. The verses quoted by Schlegel are from *Beständige Mutter oder Die Heilige Felicitas* ("The Constant Mother, or St. Felicity"), which appeared in *Deutscher Gedichte I. Teil* (1657).

> Hat Troja sonst auf nichts zu hoffen als auf ihn;
> So ist ihr Hoffen schlecht.

On the other hand, she would answer far more courageously and defiantly if her thoughts were in reverse order:

> Wenn Troja sonst auf nichts als diesen hoffen kann,
> So ist ihr Hoffen schlecht. Schau ihn doch nur recht an.
> Soll dieser Hände Kraft ein Troja wieder bauen,
> Soll er den Schutt der Stadt zu räumen sich getrauen? [3]

With most emotions, one will find that, when the last thoughts are put first and the speeches of such people read backward, a moderate emotional state turns into a very violent one which, in conformity to nature, subsides and grows weaker in the same proportion as the other grew stronger.

From this it appears all the more evident that I was not unjust in giving precedence to that explanation of similarity that speaks of a like relation among parts, for I did this lest one think that, if I had merely demanded the same quality in two similar things, it was meant to apply only to the essential part of any quality and not to its external relations.

4. *Similarity therefore exists when the same relation holds among the parts of two things. From this it necessarily follows that similarity is also present even if all relations of all the possible parts are not identical in two things.*

For we observe both the parts of the thing itself and the relations these parts have to one another only with respect to a single quality of the whole. A body has, for example, other parts

---

[3] Euripides, *The Trojan Women*, according to Martin Opitz (1597–1639):

> Just have a good look at him!
> Shall he dare to clear away the rubble of the city?
> Shall the strength of these hands rebuild Troy?
> If Troy has only him on which to place its hopes—
> Then its hopes are poor.

Schlegel rearranges the lines thus:

> If Troy has only him on which to place its hopes,
> Then its hopes are poor. Just have a good look at him.
> Shall the strength of these hands rebuild Troy?
> Shall he dare to clear away the rubble of the city?

with respect to its external form (in this case I consider only its lines and angles), others with respect to its inner structure, others with respect to the material of which it is composed, and still others with respect to its striking color. Thus, since we observe parts and relations of parts only with respect to a certain quality, it is no wonder that we also imitate them with respect to a certain quality. When all these aspects are similar to one another and when a like relation connects the parts, then the result must be an imitation if one in turn produces a like relation among parts consistently and with respect to but one quality and disregards all other relations. When one sculptures a head in stone, one does not imitate its hard or fleshy parts or its color, but only its form; and it is for this reason that poetic descriptions of a single subject can differ entirely and yet be complete. This is true because each person sees the parts with respect to a different attribute. The novelist pays attention to the limbs of a beautiful woman only insofar as they have a beautiful coloring and a size proportionate to the other parts of the body. The more thoughtful novelist, however, juxtaposes the limbs and everything else insofar as they reveal something of her emotions and insofar as her soul expresses itself through her limbs. True, one might object that an imitation of a thing that concentrates only on one quality is not an imitation of the thing itself, but merely of that quality it possesses. But this means that by the term "similarity" one would understand what I shall later describe as "the highest form of similarity." Furthermore, one would be expressing oneself in an unusual way, thereby causing the rules to be understood in a way contrary to ordinary usage. And then one would experience in many matters considerable difficulty in expressing oneself at all.

5. Even though not all the relations that we can discover among the possible parts of a thing must be identical in two objects that are to be called similar, *it is another question entirely as to whether the equality of relations among all the parts of the original and its imitation that they have in respect to a certain quality can be called similarity*. From the concept

of similarity itself, if it is examined more closely, the following offers itself as the answer: *Since similarity of original and imitation exists when there is an identical relation between the parts of the imitation and those of the original in respect to a particular quality, dissimilarity must be said to prevail when this relation is not identical. Therefore, if there were parts in the imitation that, with respect to that quality toward which the process of imitation is directed, did not have a like relation with the parts of the original, dissimilarity would prevail. But dissimilarity in those areas in which the ultimate purpose is imitation would be contrary to the aims of imitation.* A square figure, two sides and one angle of which are in proportion to those of another figure, cannot for that reason alone be called similar to it. I cannot say that a painter has painted a face similar to that of another person if he has caught only the likeness of the nose. *Yet we cannot speak of dissimilarity simply because not all parts of the original are expressed in the imitation and because no further relations are introduced into the picture in their stead—unless, that is, the imitation is thereby given an arrangement of parts differing from that of the original.* For in this latter, contrary instance, relations other than those prevailing in the original have been introduced. We cannot speak of dissimilarity, then, if the imitator has copied only an aspect or a part of the original. We do not become indignant, for example, over a bust even though the other parts of the body are not included and we get the impression that it has been separated from the trunk, for we know that the sculptor or artist wanted to represent only this part of the human figure. But, if the artist were to paint feet on it, leaving out the other parts, we would immediately become aware of the dissimilarity. However, he might express only those parts of the original from which we can recognize the object and leave us to deduce the remaining ones. In such a case, he has imitated the whole in a perfectly satisfactory manner, for the unexpressed parts are present, as it were, in the expressed ones. The imagination of the person observing the imitation comes to the assistance of the imitator and pictures the representation as complete. This is very much in agreement with Wolff's explanation that similarity is a correspondence of those parts or aspects which comprise the characteristics of two things.[4] This must suggest to us the idea of a painting in which a body is depicted only from its most advantageous side, from which we are easily able to infer what the side hidden from us is like. This fifth proposition and the preceding one will demonstrate their value and also become clearer from the following example. Günther offers no more than a single detail when he speaks of Hungary. He says

> Dort, wo der Zeiten Eigensinn,
> Die Brücke des Trajans zerdrümmert.[5]

With regard to his ultimate purpose and the feature by means of which he wants to depict Hungary (at the time when the old Roman heroes appear before him in his rapture), this land has only those attributes that are relics of classical antiquity. In his example, there are no vineyards or horses or anything else of which it might boast. The qualities Hungary would have if it were seen from the point of view of a blessed and fertile land have nothing to do with the heroes of antiquity. And so he must depict it only as a land into which the brave Romans had already extended their victories. But Hungary would then actually have more features than the bridge of Trajan! He could have described it by the armies that were

[4] The reference is to Christian Wolff (see below, p. 54, note 3), particularly to his *Vernünfftige Gedancken von Gott, der Welt, und der Seele des Menschen* ("Sensible Thoughts on God, the World, and the Human Soul," 1745). In chapter 2 of this treatise, "Von den ersten Gründen unserer Erkantniße" ("On the First Principles of Knowledge"), the concept of similarity is discussed in detail.

[5]   There, where the caprice of time
             Has destroyed Trajan's bridge.

("Trajan," or "Trianus," is the name given to Marcus Ulpius.) Christian Günther (1695–1723) was a member of the second Silesian school, a group of generally mediocre poets who wrote during the time of Gottsched. In the quality and intensity of his lyric poetry, Günther surpassed all his contemporaries. The lines quoted by Schlegel are from the poem to Prince Eugen of Savoy (lines 41–42); see below, p. 32, note 21.

there, and he could have told of the generals and their deeds. But the bridge of Trajan is enough to show that he is speaking of a land completely conquered by the Romans long before, for otherwise they would not have taken the trouble to erect such a structure there. It also reveals the era of which he is speaking by the fact that only time can destroy such a solid structure. In a word, Günther here demonstrates everything that we have said in this and the preceding sections, namely, that a description is possible without imitating all the relations of all the parts and that, in regard to a certain attribute of a subject, it is enough to indicate only those relations that contain in themselves all the others.

6. *An identical relation of parts with the parts of the original is not something that can exist per se. It presupposes a medium or primary object that exists per se and to which it adheres as something fortuitous and secondary. Thus, if I speak of an imitation, I mean thereby—and in addition to such a relation of parts to the original—also a thing possessing these parts, amidst which this identical relation can exist. Therefore, anyone who intends to imitate something must above all look for a medium in which he can find something to imitate.* Accordingly, the sculptor, for example, selects a stone from which he can carve his imitation, and the painter likewise selects his surface. Sometimes there can be things which are considered primary in regard to other things, without which the primary things cannot exist, and which nonetheless must themselves have a subject to which they are connected if they are to exist. Just as this is true, so also are there mediums of imitation which themselves require mediums in their turn. The same situation prevails in music and poetry, with their harmonious tones and metrically measured words. A tone does not exist per se, but needs a fluid medium (*Materie*) capable of taking on certain forms and sending certain waves to the ear. Nevertheless, it is a medium in regard to the various relations of tones and the various things expressed thereby.

7. *If a medium is to be suitable for imitation, it must possess that quality in respect to which I intend to imitate the*

original. In addition, it must be able to reproduce the same relations among its parts that exist among those of the original. Thus, whatever does not possess those qualities present in the original (insofar as one wants to imitate it) and whatever is not able to achieve the same relations in respect to those qualities cannot become an imitation of that model. A concrete example of this is the fact that one cannot paint a tone or imitate by means of a tone something that is merely visually evident. One should not assume that there are people who believe this possible. Yet it does happen that this principle is sometimes violated out of an excessive desire to imitate. One finds that in music the attempt is sometimes made to express the form of ocean waves by means of ascending or descending notes and the Gordian knot by means of a confusion of tones. Even height and depth, imitated in music by high and low notes, are of this sort, for height and depth are qualities belonging, not to the tones themselves, but simply to the symbols of those tones drawn on paper; and to attribute such qualities to the tones themselves betrays faulty understanding. It is an entirely different matter that in music and the spoken word one expresses what is unpleasant and annoying or pleasant and charming by a special kind of tone, for, although not everything pleasant or unpleasant can be heard, these qualities are found just as surely in tones as in other things. And so, in this regard, tones have a like quality with other things. Furthermore, it cannot be concluded that sweet and sour or tart and bitter, vividly imagined, are expressed by a particular kind of tone. In that case, the tongue does not imitate the sweet or sour or tart or bitter, but, rather, the sensation that a person has of these qualities puts the tongue in just such a physical state as exists when it tastes something having one of these qualities. Therefore, the tongue speaks as it is required to in such a situation and forms the tones that imitate, not the tone itself, but the words of the person who is tasting.

8. *The medium of an imitation is unsuitable for imitation insofar as the determination of its parts belongs by nature to the medium. Or, in a word, imitation can never extend to*

essential parts of the medium of an imitation, for the essential parts of a medium are unchangeable, and the imitation is hence incapable of assuming in its parts the same relations that exist in the original. To be sure, it is sometimes possible for the medium in which one imitates to have the same relations among its essential parts as prevail in the medium of the original, but it is not for that reason an imitation, because to this degree it is not the imitator, but nature itself, that produces the similarity. We have stated above that there can be no imitation unless there is the intent to produce something similar to another thing. The imitator deserves no credit for imitating a golden vessel in gold, and there is equally small merit in imitating in prose a speech that is itself in prose. But it also follows that no one can be censured for having imitated incorrectly if one imitates only to the degree permitted by the nature of the medium, for example, if one imitates in verse the speech of persons who after all are not in the habit of speaking naturally in verse, for verse is the poet's medium of imitation.

9. *Since imitation requires only that the parts of the imitation and their relations be like the parts of the original and their relations in respect to a certain quality and since, moreover, the essential relations among parts in the medium of the imitation do not admit of imitation, there can be in the medium of the imitation many qualities in respect of which the parts of the imitation do not stand in equal relation to the parts of the original. And despite this, the imitation can be similar to the model,* for a like relation in respect to a certain quality does not exclude dissimilarity in respect of the others. Since the artist wants to imitate only the shapes and colors of bodies as they present themselves to the eye, it is not necessary that the imitations of bodies have density as well and that they can be felt or touched as the originals are. On the contrary, the artist needs only a surface for his imitation, and soft or hard objects afford here the same resistance, namely, that which is offered by the surface on which they are painted. Consequently, it is not very sound practice to damn an imitation for

possessing qualities not present in the original, as though this were something new.

I have already given the example of verse comedy in the preceding section, and I want only to add that anyone who disapproves of verse or rhyme in comedy on the grounds given above can never accept them in another poem. The person imitated in a heroic poem speaks no more naturally in verse than does the hero in comedy, and there is something in the imitation of the former as well as the latter which is not in the original. I have felt it necessary to say this because the opponent of verse comedy whose opinion (as well as our correspondence on this subject) has not been a hindrance to either of us in our friendship has repeated his reasons and then, to make his triumph complete, assumed his proposition to be already confirmed in other respects.[6]

10. *An object has as many particular kinds of relation among its parts as it has qualities.* We have already observed that the parts of an object and their relations always have reference to a certain quality and that, in respect to every quality of an object, other parts and other relations of such parts may always be found (as we have already explained by the examples above). *The medium of the imitation can likewise contain in itself many of these qualities, in respect of which its parts are capable of those dispositions contained in the original itself. Because there is already similarity to the original when the parts of two objects have a like relation to one another in respect of a quality, there must doubtless be many similarities when the parts of these objects assume a like relationship to one another in respect of many qualities. Thus, an imitation can have many similarities to its model because it can be done in a medium whose parts are capable of many like relations with the parts of the original in respect of many qualities.* And it can have either more or fewer similarities, owing to the fact that from one similarity in the imitation another does not necessarily follow. Hence, it is a matter of

---

[6] Gottlob Benjamin Straube (see below, p. 51, note 1, and Introduction, p. xxii) is the opponent of verse comedy to whom Schlegel refers.

chance whether more or fewer similarities arise. *The multiplicity of similarities determines their stage, or degree,* and, since there can be greater or fewer similarities in an imitation, *they can have degrees in their imitations.* To illustrate this, I need only the example of painting. I can draw a thing simply with regard to the form that presents itself to the eye. This is a similarity. Then I can add light and shadow. This is the other similarity. And, finally, I can add to these two similarities that of color. Thus I have here three distinct stages of similarity. And one can distinguish many other similarities in the presentation of a play. One can express in a work the imitation of human customs simply through the words by which the persons make themselves known; or one can imitate the stress of speech manifest when a poem is read; or one can imitate the gestures, clothing, and setting.

11. *Where there is no intent to produce similarity, there is no imitation. A thing is therefore imitated only insofar as there is an intent to make it similar to something else; and imitation must be judged solely according to the intent if one is to determine whether the imitation is good. Therefore, the choice of the degree and medium of imitation—as well as of the original itself—is a matter of indifference.* One need on that account have no fear that people will make use of this fact by denying their intent to imitate if the imitation is poor, because there are means of discovering intentions. Besides, anyone who wanted to make use of this advantage would not thereby be freed from all reproach, for we could still call him to account for not having had a higher purpose. And so, whereas he ought to have justified his work, he will have to defend his aims instead.

We can judge the imitator's intent all the more easily because similarity itself cannot be the ultimate aim of imitation, but must be brought about merely as a means to an end. And, once we know what this more distant end is, we can only decide whether the imitator has chosen the degree and the model that satisfy this aim. Just as a medium that does neither more nor less than what is demanded by the ultimate purpose may be called a perfect choice, so, too, is an imitation perfect that does not go beyond its purpose or fail to attain it. It ought to be more difficult to divine this ultimate purpose, but for that one needs nothing more than rules supplied him by his good sense.

One sees, too, that perhaps these things—namely, medium, model, and the degree of imitation—though they be arbitrary, are in certain cases already given a priori (and, to be sure, either one or all three of them). In the case of the artist, the given medium of imitation is always that which is appropriate to his art. One cannot expect music to be the medium of the poet's imitation, nor can one demand of a musician that he imitate in unarranged tones and without harmony or that the heroes he imitates should only talk and not sing.

12. *The greatest degree of similarity prevails when all the relations of the parts of the one are identical to all the relations of the parts of the other. Thus, the greatest degree of similarity is achieved when the imitation and model are identical.* This greatest degree of similarity is in itself impossible because two things cannot be one and the same. Still, we need this proposition for what is to follow. For the moment, we shall conclude only that, *in order to attain the greatest degree of similarity, it is also necessary that the medium of the imitation have the same arrangement* (Bestimmungen) *in its nature as does the medium of the original.* But it has been proven above that imitation does not extend to the nature of the medium, either because the medium cannot be made similar to the original or because it is by nature already similar to it. *It follows from this that the greatest degree of imitation is distinct from the greatest degree of similarity. The former is reached when all possible relations in the parts of the imitation correspond with the original.* In painting, for example, the greatest degree of imitation is attained when design, shadow, and color correspond to those of the original, for nothing more of a body can be put on a surface. Thus, if there are two mediums, both equally incapable of taking on a number of similarities through imitation, the original can be imi-

tated to the highest degree in both, whereas the degree of imitation according to the number of similarities still differs.

13. Whoever undertakes to imitate something tries to see to it that the parts of the imitation correspond to the parts of the original. *He must therefore be able to distinguish the parts of the original from one another.* In this connection, we see a special value in poetry in that it can aid philosophy also in training us to form clear concepts of things and to observe in them what it is that distinguishes them from others. The average person names many things in nature about whose parts he has never concerned himself, but a poet can never imitate them or, as is customarily said, describe them poetically unless he has distinguished their attributes and knows more about an object than the fact that it is a flower or an animal or the like. What one generally calls poetic verve or poetic style is based on the fact that one does not describe an object with the mere words that define it directly themselves, but rather with the characteristics of that object. This can be seen from the well-known example which Boileau sometimes quoted from himself. It is not an imitation or a representation of old age when I say, "I am sixty-eight years old"; but there is imitation when I say, as Boileau does,

> Mais aujourd' hui qu' enfin la vieillesse venue
> Sous mes faux cheveux blonds déjà toute chenue
> A jetté sur ma tête avec ses doigts pesans,
> Onze lustres complets surchargés de trois ans.[7]

Professor Gottsched rightly puts these words of praise in the mouth of Poetry so that man can be taught to observe nature. He shows that he himself does this when he has Poetry say to man:

---

[7] See Introduction, pp. xiii–xiv.
> But today, when finally old age has come
> Under my false blond hair, already completely gray,
> And has thrown upon my head, with heavy fingers,
> Eleven lustra, overburdened with three [more] years.

This passage, not identified by Schlegel, is found in *Épitre* X (1695), *Vie et portrait de l'auteur, à mes vers*, lines 25–28.

> Schaue, wie sich Haupt und Glied
> Fleisch und Bein so künstlich fügen,
> Wie sich Flächs und Sähne zieht,
> Wie die vollen Muskeln liegen.
> Gieb auf deiner Adern Menge
> Und des Blutes Kreislauf acht,
> Den das Herz mit reger Macht,
> Durch sein spritzendes Gedränge,
> In die kleinsten Zäsern treibt,
> Daß kein Pünktchen saftlos bleibt.[8]

When Dr. Haller says that here is a lofty mountain from which a stream plunges down to form a waterfall, he is offering a poetic description capable of giving us the clearest idea of these things:

> Hier zeigt ein steiler Berg die mauer gleichen Spitzen,
> Ein Waldstrom eilt dadurch und stürzet Fall auf Fall,
> Der dickbeschäumte Fluß dringt durch der Felsen Ritzen
> Und schießt mit jäher Kraft weit über ihren Wall.
> Das dünne Wasser theilt des tiefen Falles Eile,
> In der verdickten Luft schwebt ein bewegtes Grau.
> Ein Regenbogen strahlt durch die zerstäubten Theile;
> Und das entfernte Thal trinkt ein beständig Thau.[9]

---

[8] See how head and limbs
Flesh and bones are so artfully joined,
How tendons and sinews extend,
And how the full muscles lie;
Observe your numerous arteries
And the circulation of blood
Which the heart, with zealous strength,
Drives through its surging maze
Into the smallest fibers,
That not a single spot remains dry.

Schlegel does not locate these lines in the voluminous works of Gottsched.

[9] Here a steep mountain shows its wall-like peaks,
A forest stream rushes through and plunges from cascade to cascade,
The thick-foamed river pushes through the rocky clefts
And with sudden force shoots far over the rocky edges.
The sheet of water divides the rush of the long fall,
A grayness hovers in the spray-filled air.
A rainbow shines through the spray,
And the distant valley drinks unceasing dew.

Albrecht Haller (1708–1788) is best known for the long descriptive poem *Die Alpen* ("The Alps," 1729), from which these lines (351–358) are taken.

Poetry teaches man, especially in the images it gives him, to recognize clearly the quality of human emotions. Von Hagedorn's descriptions of Agnes and Laurette illustrate clearly that poetic descriptions that seem to others to have been merely for the sake of arousing an emotion (which assails the human heart often enough as it is) are useful in ethics as well.[10]

14. *Where there is a like relation between two things, there is of necessity order, for order means precisely an agreement or correspondence in the relation of things. Thus, imitation necessarily brings about order* by virtue of the fact that it produces agreement between the relations of parts of an imitation and those of the original. Order also arises even if the original does not have internal order. Let us assume a model whose parts and connections do not have the slightest correspondence; now let us call these parts A, B, C, and D, and let us represent them in the imitation with a, b, c, and d. The ratios will then be $A:a = B:b = C:c = D:d$; and we shall observe a sufficient degree of correspondence (or whatever we choose to call order) among the diverse things. This deduction applies to all observations on similarity.

Even Aristotle has said the same thing of metaphorical language that I am saying here of imitation.[11] If I call old age the evening of life, the similarity between old age and evening can be reduced to the conclusion: old age is to life as evening is to day. And, in order to show that everything in a mathematical relation or equation can be extended to other things, I can also conclude thus: as old age is in proportion to evening, so is life in proportion to day. We draw such conclusions in every

---

[10] Friedrich von Hagedorn (1708–1754), lyric poet and author of fables, was one of the leading representatives of German rococo literature. The reference to Agnes and Laurette, not further identified by Schlegel, is presumably to the poem "Laurette," which is based on one of the tales in Boccaccio's *Decameron* (Fourth Story of the Seventh Day) and to the poem *Paulus Purganti und Agnese,* based on the verse narrative, *Paulo Purganti,* by the English poet Matthew Prior. The description of Agnes is found in the latter poem.

[11] For Aristotle on metaphorical language, see *Poetics* 21.

poetic description if we are but careful to observe. However, we do not distinguish these conclusions clearly. I shall illustrate this with an example taken from Dr. Haller and containing both similarities and dissimilarities. When I hear the word "autumn," my imagination forms a concept or idea which, to be sure, is unclear, but in which autumn's parts (or whatever can be distinguished in it) are contained. This idea becomes a model (*Vorbild*) as soon as I hear another description of autumn.

> Bald wenn der trübe Herbst die falben Blätter pflücket.[12]

I imagine to myself the picture that this line has awakened in me apart from the idea of autumn; I compare it to the idea and find that the quality of the weather and the quality of the leaves have the same relation in the idea of autumn, in autumn itself, and to each other as the impressions aroused in me by the words *trüb* and *falb* [13] have to the weather and the leaves in the imitation. I find, further, that the falling of leaves in the model [i.e., nature] does not have the same relation to the leaves as the impression which the word *pflücken* [14] (as used for autumn) has to the leaves in the imitation. In the former, I notice a gentle release; in the latter, on the other hand, a forceful one, and this causes me to react with surprise to a comparison of imitation and original. And I find that the melancholy of autumn has no relation at all to the falling of leaves, inasmuch as there is nothing in the former that could be explained by the latter. We see, then, that a correspondence of relations is lacking because agreement is present in the imitation but not in the model.

And when I hear,

> Und sich die kühle Luft in graue Nebel kleidt,[15]

---

[12] Soon, when dismal autumn plucks the faded leaves.
—Haller, *Die Alpen*, line 211.

[13] "Dismal" and "faded."
[14] "To pluck."
[15] And the cool air clothes itself in gray mists,
—Haller, *Die Alpen*, line 212.

I observe that coolness and air have the same relation in the imitation as air and its particular quality in the original and that the same applies to the gray fog. But I am again surprised when I see that cool air and fog do not have the same relation in the original as they do in the imitation, which was inspired by the word *kleiden*.[16] For, in the imitation, the fog moves about in the air, whereas in the original it becomes mingled with it. Anyone who doubts that a person draws all these conclusions and examines all these relations should simply test himself to see whether he does not have two concepts when he reads a description. And then he should observe whether he has a completely different sensation when he hears: "it is autumn." This, too, is nothing new insofar as we also compare what is said of a thing to the thing itself when we are investigating the truth. We can perceive even more markedly that we must inevitably come to such conclusions (insofar as it is our intention to examine ourselves) when we hear a riddle. A riddle offers a representation (*Bild*) to my thoughts, to be sure, but not its model. And so I attempt to search for a model among the concepts I have gained; I constantly compare all parts of the riddle to my concepts until I find one that agrees with it in all parts. But then a riddle is nothing more than the imitation of something that I leave to others to guess. Would we want to find out after considerable time whether something incorrect was said when we could find out immediately by openly drawing these conclusions for ourselves?

15. *When I observe order, I have a sense of pleasure; and so, when I observe a similarity of imitation to original, I react in the same way.* It is the kind of pleasure that arises from the nature of imitation. I do not by any means deny that there can also be many other kinds of pleasure arising from imitation, but I want now to speak of only one kind, namely, that which can most clearly be shown to be derived from imitation; that which is alone inevitably evoked by contemplation of imitation and not by any of its incidental aspects; indeed, that which goes so far that in our explanation of it we cannot even

[16] "To clothe."

appeal to human nature, but must recognize that it comes from the nature of a thinking creature in general. Further, it has been my sole purpose here to prove that pleasure arises from imitation. I shall reserve for the next section my comments on this pleasure and the rules for attaining it.

II. ON THE NATURE AND RULES OF IMITATION INSOFAR AS ITS PRIMARY AIM IS PLEASURE

The last proposition of the preceding part is that imitation affords pleasure. I confess that many people have wondered why I wanted to prove this and, moreover, why I did it in so detailed a way as to use almost the entire first part in laying the groundwork for this proof (which is somewhat deep and annoying because of my detailed explanation as to how pleasure arises). But I, for my part, wonder even more that there are people who endeavor to produce this pleasure but are nevertheless sufficiently indifferent not to learn how it originates. For such knowledge could make their endeavors easier and more certain of success. When we show how effect is linked to cause, we show at the same time the means for achieving this effect. But ought anyone be annoyed when one shows him the means of attaining his ultimate purpose? Now, pleasure is, to be sure, not *the* ultimate purpose of all imitation, but it is nevertheless the goal of that imitation with which I am dealing particularly and which is the basis of the various arts. And so one cannot investigate sufficiently the sources of pleasure. Whoever reproaches me for having dealt with the origin of pleasure in a not-altogether-entertaining way will also have to censure those who write about music for the fact that their treatises do not have any such agreeable sound to our ears as has the harmony of tones about which they write. I shall continue, then, in my attempt to give the rules and means for arousing this pleasure; and perhaps in this part I shall be more successful in showing the reader in more agreeable fashion the way to give others pleasure through imitation. The entrance to this "way"—which, like a theater entrance, has something dark and drab about it—seems now to have been put behind us with the first part of my treatise.

16. *Since imitation is a cause of pleasure, and pleasure an effect of imitation, there is no doubt that pleasure may be considered the chief function of imitation.* Pleasure is doubtless one of the most natural purposes of imitation, since the latter is a perfect means for attaining the former and also since it necessarily produces the former, not by chance but inevitably and by its very nature. *One customarily uses imitation for two further purposes, namely, either to instruct*—so that the original is grasped as fully as possible from its imitation—*or to deceive*—so that the imitation is taken for the thing it represents. The first is the purpose of history; the second, of lies. Such diverse and totally unrelated things produce imitation in order to use it both to teach and to suppress truth. The historian wants to instruct his reader and give him a conception of a past event. He chooses the words that are the very clearest indication of what happened. These words excite in the reader ideas of the things for which they stand. The historian would not be content with these ideas of a thing, but would show his reader the thing itself if this were possible.

The poet wants to please the reader by means of a comparison between imitation and original. He chooses every means he can find to make the similarity of his imitation evident. He is so far from wanting to show the reader the thing itself rather than an imitation of it that he would consider his purpose false if he were to attempt to do so. Thus, when two persons imitate the same thing, that which may be considered a fault in the one may be cause for praise in the other. The historian and the poet can imitate the Battle of Pharsalus or Henry the Great's deeds.[17] Their purpose differs only in that

[17] The battle of Pharsalus (or Pharsalia), 48 B.C., is generally considered the decisive battle between Caesar and Pompey, for it made Caesar master of the Roman world. The Roman writer Lucan wrote an epic poem on the subject.

Of the many European sovereigns named Henry, two Henry IV's were

they employ like means in a different manner. This is the kind of imitation whose chief aim is to instruct, and those who call all kinds of writing imitation and consider every writer a learned painter are using the term in this meaning. However, we shall distinguish between these two types of imitation because their functions are changed by their final aim. A writer who imitates in order to instruct cannot simply follow the rules designed to promote pleasure.

As far as deception is concerned, many have found it so pleasing that little is wanting for them to trace pleasure arising from imitation back to it. It is not so much that they have believed that all painting and imitation bring about delight through the sense of order that one is made to feel or through a comparison of imitation and original; it is rather that they have thought painting and imitation achieve this through pleasing deception and the confusion of imitation and original in the reader's or viewer's mind. It cannot be denied that what they call deception and, much more than that (to speak according to their opinion), what they ought to call the discovery of deception is sometimes bound up with pleasure. But this pleasure is so incidental that it is inferior to the pleasure evoked by the harmony of parts, and it arises only because the discovery of deception noticeably aids in perceiving an exact correspondence of parts in the imitation with those in the original. Let us say, for example, that a man is watching a play. The players' art delights him so much that he takes the disguised persons for real heroes and their sufferings for true suffering. A moment later, he remembers his error and is pleased to have been deceived in such an entertaining way.

Strictly speaking, there is, in my opinion, no pleasant deception. A deception or an error is always testimony to a weakness in our ability to understand, and no matter how sugar-coated

---

called "the Great": Henry of Navarre (1553–1610), king of France, and Henry IV (1056–1106), the Holy Roman emperor who was excommunicated by the pope and forced to do penance at Canossa (in 1077). It is not clear to which king Schlegel is referring, for both may be said to have performed "deeds."

one or the other may be, they make us more abashed than amused. To be sure, our discovery of the deception could satisfy our curiosity, but only rarely does it outweigh the stigma of error, with which it is so intimately connected by virtue of the pleasure we take in learning something. In short, this discovery of error, which has been called a pleasant and stimulating deception, brings about a kind of pleasure much too bitter for one to be able to explain the kind of pleasure arising from the imitation with which we are concerned here. The only things that could render this deception pleasant on our discovery of it would be the facts that it is an incontestable sign of great similarity between imitation and original and that we perceive all the more distinctly the order and perfection arising from our confusion of the two. Such would be the means by which one could show this pleasant deception from its most attractive side. But, according to my feeling—and in point of fact—*I find in the most exact of imitations a greater tendency to deceive than an actual deception,* that is to say, so long as the imitation still affords satisfaction in this exact form.

A child who has been taken to a comedy sees Molière's Lisette appear on stage.[18] When she is administered a beating, the child weeps along with her and feels a real, not a pleasant, sadness. Thereupon it is said that Lisette's tears are not real and her beating not seriously administered. This is enough to stop the child's tears, but not enough to arouse its pleasure. A person sees a painted head from a distance and takes it to be a stone sculpture. He goes up to it and learns that he was mistaken. To those who are with him he says nothing about

[18] In *L'Amour médecin* ("Love's the Best Doctor"), Lisette is maid to Lucinde. Although there is no indication in the play itself (including the scanty stage directions) that Lisette is beaten, Schlegel's reference may nevertheless be correct. As Molière himself says, "Very much depends on performance. . . . One would wish that works of this kind might always be seen with the embellishment which they enjoy when performed before his Majesty, where they appear to much greater advantage" ("Foreword to the Reader"). And so it is probable that Schlegel saw such an "embellished" production.

his error and is ashamed of having been deceived. We see here the effect of a genuine deception. Now let us compare this to the feeling aroused by what critics call a pleasant deception, but which I, on the other hand, wanted merely to call our tendency to be deceived—a tendency related to the pleasure of actually having avoided such an error.

17. I made the preceding remarks, not only in order that we recognize the possibility of this purpose in imitation (namely, that of pleasure's arising directly from our perception of similarity), but also that we may distinguish this purpose, in respect of which I have examined imitation, from its other purposes. I shall now undertake to prove something that we do not derive merely from the nature of imitation, but that requires the help of experience. My thesis is, namely, that *this pleasure is the true purpose of the kind of imitation we encounter in the arts.*

All pleasure belongs to the things one seeks for their own sake. Because our happiness consists in the union of all possible kinds of pleasure, each single pleasure bears a direct influence on this union. If something pleases us, it is pointless to ask why we seek this pleasure. *Any pleasure, therefore, that arises from the nature of a thing may be presumed to be the ultimate purpose of that thing;* and it has, more than anything else, the right to be regarded as the *raison d'être* of that pleasure-giving thing in the world. Its claim to this is so powerful that we should not give credence to anyone who tried to tell us that something other than pleasure was its most important purpose—unless we have before our eyes the clearest evidence that its originator and creator had something else in mind.

One customarily cites two things as being the chief functions of poetry—pleasure and instruction. This is not without its reasons, as we shall have occasion to mention later. But, when we ask which of the two is the primary purpose, *I must confess*—and let the most rigid moralists look as sour as they like—*that pleasure takes precedence over instruction* and that the poet who pleases and does not instruct is to be more highly esteemed as a poet than the one who instructs and does not please. In this connection, we do not need to pose any questions of conscience as to *whether the writer and the reader of a poem look or wish for something more than to please and be pleased.* We can see clearly enough from their actions that this is not just the wish of the poet alone; the very same intention has been admitted with no hypocrisy by readers and spectators since antiquity. Among the poets of classical antiquity, Anacreon is greater than Theognis, and the gilded poems of Pythoras cut a poor figure when compared to the venomous ones of Ovid. I have never heard anyone call Cato, with his moral pronouncements, a better poet than Catullus, with his frivolous wit. This shows how far the purpose of instruction in poetry lags behind that of pleasure. If one were to say that *men often use the best things in a perverse way and make the subsidiary purpose the main one, we should have to grant that this is true; but no one who uses a thing for an improper purpose will for that reason admit that his purpose is wrong.* On the contrary, he cloaks his improper intentions with the good appearance of an aim quite other than that which he actually has in mind. One holds honorary offices, for example, in order to feather one's nest; but one says, at least, that the primary purpose is to promote the common welfare. *Should poets alone, then, possess so little cunning that, if poetry's main purpose is supposed to be instruction, they do not say so publicly and unanimously?* But, granted that there are poets whose main purpose is to instruct their readers or who at least proclaim this intention to all the world in order to set themselves above the ordinary run of poets, *is instruction for that reason the primary aim of all poetry—I will not say of imitation—because it is the ultimate aim of some poets?* Artists sometimes depict battles, and sculptors heroes, in order to keep their memory alive for posterity. But we do not on that account conclude that history is the ultimate purpose of painting or that sculpture was invented so that we might after some years have a notion of how Lysander or some other Greek general looked.[19] The primary aim of art is a necessary effect of art; the primary aim of the artist, however, can often consist in something quite incidental to art but connected to it by the poet.

18. *Imitation whose aim is pleasure attains its end when similarity and, hence, also the order that creates it are perceived. It is therefore necessary, not only to imitate, but to do so in such a way that similarity of imitation to model is perceived* and, moreover, is perceived by the one in whom we seek to arouse pleasure. Order that we do not perceive is the same as no order. *From this it follows that we must employ every means at our disposal to present clearly* to those for whom we imitate *both imitation and original. We must therefore refrain from making our imitations obscure and confused.* Sculptors, artists, musicians, and poets can heed or disregard this rule, each in his special way and according to the particular nature of his art. If we place pictures far above the eyes of the viewer or paint descriptions on some elevated place so faintly and small that he can see but little of them, or if we draw the subject in any way that would make it impossible for him to recognize adequately what is being depicted—even though it corresponds fully to the original—it is obvious that the purpose of art is not thereby achieved.

Phidias' carving, which he made large and rough so that it could be seen clearly from its height, illustrates the degree to which the rule of clarity governs other rules of art.[20] If, in music and poetry, I conceal nature beneath too many decorations and figures, I likewise offend against clarity; and a poet in particular finds many other ways of being unclear and inhibiting the pleasure that the beauty of his images (*Bilder*)

---

[19] Lysander was a Spartan general who rose to eminence during the Peloponnesian War. His decisive victory in the Hellespont had the effect of ending the war.

[20] Phidias (born *ca.* 490 B.C.), considered the greatest Greek sculptor, was a native of Athens. Of his numerous works, the enormous statue (almost forty feet high) of Athene in the Parthenon is perhaps the most notable. Schlegel's reference to Phidias' carving is probably to this statue.

are not to blame if we do not manage to afford pleasure to countless people. The great difference between desiring the approbation of many people and wanting to give them pleasure can be seen from this fact: every poet is highly honored as having given pleasure to the fair sex, but he will not boast much of their approval in general and apart from that of individual persons among them. This is true because many such persons cannot know what true and constant pleasure is able to do.

It is evident from the above that whoever imitates something should endeavor to give pleasure to as many as possible, unless he has a special object in mind. *But it is impossible to please everyone because there are too many prejudiced people. Therefore, the surest way to please the greatest number is to try to delight the discerning ones.* The pleasure the imitator thereby creates will be all the more estimable because the discerning person is more deserving of it than the ignorant one. *In respect to art, a discerning person is one who has no prejudices about that art and who possesses a sufficient degree of sensitivity for its works to make an impression on him.* The untrained person of intelligence is as important in this regard as the learned one. And the connoisseur is as worthy of pleasure as a person who does not understand art. The only valid distinction is that made by the vivacity of an unspoiled imagination. *It therefore follows that, in imitating, both original and imitation should be of such a nature—unless the imitator already has other, specific purposes—that they can make a universal impression without presupposing the existence of certain ideas on the part of a particular class of people* and also that they should not be too difficult for people with trained and untrained minds alike, but should serve both at the same time.

20. *Order that we do not perceive cannot afford us pleasure. Yet, we do not perceive the order and similarity of imitation and original if we (whom the representation is supposed to please) have in our minds an idea differing from that of the imitator. In such a case, the pleasure sought cannot be at-*

tained. We see this clearly in classical Greek poetry. Those inadequately acquainted with classical antiquity cannot find pleasure in this poetry, for they either have a concept of ancient heroes and customs different from that of the Greek poets or they do not get the descriptions of these things in their proper intensity, but only in translations, which weaken or distort their characteristics. In our time, we have created a new Achilles, a new Hippolytus—in short, completely new heroes who have a great deal of the nature of great men of our time and are merely put into classical costume. Whoever demands that poems of classical antiquity be identical to our ideas is demanding that the imitation precede the model, for the poems were written several thousand years ago, whereas our ideas did not come to be until modern times. From this I conclude: *whoever imitates must be guided by the ideas of those whom the imitation is intended to please;* that is to say, if their ideas of the original do not correspond to what the original really is, the imitator may no longer take for his model the thing itself, but the ideas of those for whose pleasure he is making the imitation. The latter, then, must be dissimilar to the subject if it is to be more in harmony with the concepts of that subject. One might object that the result would be a spurious pleasure, because the imitation is based on apparent rather than true similarity. Such an objection, however, is easily put aside because the comparison of imitation and original is made in the imagination. The original is therefore not the subject itself, but its concept and image.

Because an imitation is usually only a concept, I should be comparing two totally dissimilar things if I were to liken the concept to the thing itself. If, therefore, the imitation corresponds only to the concept of the original in the minds of those for whose pleasure we imitate, it can never produce an apparent pleasure. For, supposing that the person who has felt this pleasure then changes his idea of the model, he is still constantly aware of the fact that the imitator has yielded to his prejudice and has imitated faithfully, whereas he himself merely had an inaccurate idea from the start.

Although we now have a completely different view of the world from that held in Virgil's and Ovid's time, we still find pleasure in their descriptions. We still delight in reading their depictions of the omnipotence of gods in whom we no longer believe, because we know that they represent perfectly the concepts of their times. But, if a modern poet were to use the same subjects, he would disregard the rules to the same degree that the earlier poets followed them—unless, that is, he took his subjects from such a time and treated them in such a manner that, in thinking of the classical age, we would also unwittingly accept their concepts and believe the poet to be of that age. If the imitator accommodated himself to the ideas of his critics, readers, or spectators (or for whomever he produced his representations), many unjust and premature judgments containing occasional accusations of unnaturalness on the part of the imitator would disappear. For example, who has ever heard a great man speak consistently in the manner of a king or hero of a tragedy? But would we on that account claim that Racine is unnatural because he never wrote a line which does not contain a noble thought? And would we speak of unnaturalness when the host of superfluous words and speeches that inevitably creep into everyday speech (even that of great men) was banished from every tragedy? Or when not a single base word was permitted in tragedy, even though history could prove that a great man had uttered it?

Tragedy imitates the ideas that the majority of people—the more intelligent ones as well—have of great men, especially of dead heroes. Death and time have for the most part taken from these men the things that made them like other people; there is nothing left but those characteristics by which we recognize their superiority over other men. So everyone from childhood on forms a nobler conception of their manner of thinking and speaking than truth demands. Even living heroes avoid social relations to the degree necessary to keep men from getting to know any side which does not show them speaking nobly and of important matters. Tragedy, then, imitates these concepts and can therefore deal only with the connection between noble thoughts and deeds. It is to be praised for this because it not only satisfies our ideas, but also sustains the respect we owe kings.

With this, I believe that I have proved and explained something that seems at first glance utterly false: to imitate well, one must sometimes make the imitation dissimilar to the model.

21. *Things not similar to each other per se can nevertheless attain similarity if we have a concept of one or the other that differs from the true nature of that thing.* In the preceding section, we have been concerned with this possibility insofar as one has a concept of the model that is not identical to it. *This applies also if the imitation is completely dissimilar, not only to the original, but also to the concept one normally has of it. However, such an imitation can still be good if it creates, under certain conditions, an image in our minds similar to the original.*

The first such kind of imitation is optical illusion and anything else that may be termed artistic deception of the senses. In short, I am referring to the things that create a concept in our minds similar to that made by a certain model, not by virtue of their nature, but accidentally; that is, if they are seen in a certain position and from a certain angle or if they are viewed from a certain distance. A tablet on whose narrow, obliquely raised surfaces are painted nothing but indiscernible dots that, when seen from a certain side and at a particular angle, form a complete painting or, as it is customarily called, a *tabula strigata,* is a good and proper imitation. This holds true even if the subject it is supposed to represent does not bear the slightest resemblance to it in terms of that subject's actual composition. To this kind of imitation belongs the theatrical stabbing, in which the dagger seems to penetrate the breast while actually only passing between the arms. But such imitations can be made only when the imitation is truly external and perceived by our senses. They are not possible at all when the representation is formed in our imagination, as is the case with epic poetry, where the representation and the image we have of it in our thoughts are one and the same.

On the other hand, with these latter and with all imitations in general, another faultless imitation can be achieved, namely, that which is not very noticeable and which can be discovered only through most exacting scrutiny. It is often neither possible nor desirable to achieve perfect similarity between objects. But the pleasure aroused in discovering similarities serves to tone down many dissimilarities, if they are well concealed, from the viewer. Also, two things may for that reason seem similar to each other even if many of their features do not correspond, for not everything can be evident in the images that overload, as it were, a person's mind. We see that, because this impression of dissimilarity results from the inattentiveness of others, it cannot be allowed in greater measure than what we would expect to find among the most attentive people. Of course, it remains a deviation from the rule and hence not permissible unless another rule happens to demand it. This is so in order that those who wish to examine the imitation more closely will not notice such a dissimilarity without discovering at the same time a reason to justify it. We see, therefore, that unnoticable dissimilarity does not prevent us from finding things similar even when they are not. A painting is considered similar to its original even when it is viewed from an improper angle. A theater is set up from one angle of vision and yet must be clear to many hundreds of people at the same time. And who can find in poetry two word portraits that are not dissimilar in some way although both may bear a likeness to the person depicted? The Electra of Sophocles, Euripides, Aeschylus, and, among the moderns, Crébillon, are utterly different representations. Yet one cannot say of any one of them that they fail to observe character faithfully. Racine's Achilles is not the Achilles of Corneille, not to mention many other examples that clearly demonstrate the application of our rule and show when it is permissible to make an imitation dissimilar to its model.

22. *A prerequisite for pleasure arising from imitation is the comparison of imitation and original in the minds of those whom the imitation is designed to affect. Consequently, there must be two conceptions in their imagination—one of the original and one of the imitation. If one of these is missing, the entire effect of the imitation will be lost.*This can happen:

(1) *If the imitation is so like its original in all respects that the mind is unable to distinguish them* and considers them the same. I have dealt with this in my essay in defense of verse comedy. In the opinion of some informed friends, there is one objection at least that I ought to raise here: Is such a likeness of imitation and original possible? The philosophical proposition that two things cannot be exactly alike has no bearing here, for they can at least give the appearance of being completely identical. In a comparison of things, the mind pays no attention to slight, imperceptible differences; they are discovered only through exact scrutiny. Moreover, our concepts of the original are indefinite in many details because they are made up of general concepts. Hence, as soon as the mind perceives something that appears to fit the general concept completely, it no longer takes it to be an imitation, but the original. For there is no pleasure to be derived in discovering that a thing is similar to itself! Nor can there be any sense of the pleasure brought about by imitation when I see that one egg is like another or that a tree has the true characteristics of trees.

We find an example of such a natural imitation in faces in which, to the great annoyance of the audience, one cannot distinguish the real from the imitated. A mime, let us say, is supposed to portray a person in great rage. Instead of remaining within the limts of imitated rage and portraying it with understanding, he shows all the characteristics of a genuinely insane person. He is not content merely to rage excessively on the stage; he runs among the audience and carries out his various excesses there, causing the spectators to think that he has become truly mad. And no one in the audience would be grateful to him for this deception.

(2) The second instance in which the main effect of imita-

tion can be lost through lack of an essential concept in the minds of the listeners, spectators, or readers occurs *when these latter have no concept of the model.* A portrait's greatest beauty is lost to all those who do not know the subject and is beautiful only insofar as it bears similarity to a person in general. A poet must therefore know his readers' concepts if his imitation is not to be for naught or, as it were, for another age. The examples and metaphors one used to take from old travel descriptions of Indian fauna and flora—above all anything that had an exotic name—are most unsuitable for imitation. The description of a hen, a female animal,

> Das von dem leichten Volk, so sich in Feldern kleidet,
> Des Kammes kronen gleiche Zier
> Die Wachsamkeit (die Phyllis nie beneidet)
> Und treue Dummheit unterscheidet;
> Das blinden Aberwitz von guten Männern borgt,
> Und Junge fremder Art, als seine Zucht versorgt,[24]

is worth a hundred times more than the depiction of a phoenix, even though in comparison to the phoenix a hen belongs to the plebeians of poultry. The same may also be said of learned descirptions in poems written (in the opinion of their authors), not for the pleasure of the learned, but to delight all classes of people. In the reader's mind, the original is lacking, and therefore the imitations are without force and serve only to annoy him. The most natural description of a pagan god can no longer have the effect today that it had in

[24] The description of a hen is from "Die Henne und der Smaragd" ("The Hen and the Emerald"), one of the *Fabeln und Erzählungen* ("Fables and Tales") of Friedrich von Hagedorn. The 1757 edition of the collected works offers a variant reading of the fifth line: "Das blinde Gütigkeit . . ." instead of "Das blinden Aberwitz . . . ," i.e., "which blind benevolence" instead of the dubious and altogether inappropriate "which blind conceit."

> Which is distinguished from the flighty folk who clad
>   themselves in feathers
> By the crownlike ornament of the comb,
> By vigilance (Phyllis never envied this),
> And by faithful stupidity;
> Which borrows blind benevolence from good men
> And cares for the young of a brood other than its own.

Virgil's time; it seems to have been made only for lovers of antiquity. To a person without learning, the description,

> Wenn holdes Weigern, sanftes Zwingen,
> Verliebter Diebstahl, reizend Singen,
> Mit Wollust beyder Herz beräuscht;
> Wenn der verwirrte Blick der Schönen,
> Ihr schwimmend Aug voll seichter Thränen
> Was sie verweigert, heimlich heischt,[25]

will be much more charming than Venus' girdle and the description Homer gives of it.

But from this we cannot conclude that things our readers have not actually seen ought not to be imitated. If they are familiar only with the parts of a thing, they will be able to construct it in their minds. Nor can it be concluded that we may not describe a new and hitherto-unknown species of something; on the contrary, the reader's pleasure is infinitely heightened when we acquaint him with something new—either in nature or in the realm of representations—by showing him a copy or imitation of it. We also increase his knowledge thereby, especially if the strange, unknown things have something wondrous and attractive about them.

From this it follows that we should either choose subjects to imitate that are already part of the concepts of those we are attempting to please, or, in those cases where we have reason to imitate unknown things, we should seek ways and means to give a concept of the original along with its representation. At this moment, three such means occur to me as particularly useful in poetry—whereby I do not mean to deny that there can be others as well. One is to give a description of something along with its representation as an aid to forming a concept of it. An example of this is to characterize the person whose

---

[25] When charming refusal, gentle forcing,
amorous theft, delightful struggling
enrapture both hearts in bliss;
when the disconcerted glance of the fair maiden,
her moist eyes filled with insipid tears,
secretly demands what she declines,

Schlegel fails to identify these lines, presumably by a contemporary or late-seventeenth-century German poet.

would otherwise awaken in the minds of his readers. *For everything that causes the reader's attention to flag, detracts from the similarity of representation to model, or causes the latter to make a weaker impression than that which is necessary to perceive its beauty is for these very reasons reprehensible and deserving of the epithet "obscure."* A poet's clarity thus extends far beyond the careful and felicitous combining of words, although this in particular is very necessary. A poem is never read to exercise one's intellect by creating order out of a confusion of words, but rather to compare one concept to another. This is especially true in view of the fact that the difficulty of sentence structure often causes us to err and at first give a wrong meaning to a word until we can later think of the right one. But this kind of error is diametrically opposed to pleasure; not only do we see disorder instead of order in the images, but on discovering our error we have a feeling of displeasure that is inseparably bound up with the conviction that we have erred. By the same token, and to my mind to an even greater degree, two other things are opposed to clarity. They consist less in a confused arrangement than in an inadequacy or a misuse of words and are consequently all the more faulty in exerting a greater influence on the subject matter itself. I am referring to ambiguity and vagueness of expression. The first entices the reader into missing the true features of an imitation and imagining others instead; the second causes him to lose such features entirely or to search long and vainly for them.

Confused word order is the error common to inferior poets, who from forced scrupulousness seem to look only for the thoughts and images and to care little for the words themselves. Similarly, the two faults of ambiguity and uncertainty of expression are found in facile poets. Those of whom one says that they write with greatest facility sometimes seem to me more obscure than those who write with least facility. For a style that is determined to be facile sometimes finds the words before the thoughts themselves, leaving the reader to lend *his* thoughts to the poet. Or such poets choose more sonorous words than those that express the subject better. In this regard Günther in particular seems to me much more often unclearer than poets accused of lack of clarity due to an unpolished style.

Someone before me has already commented on the following lines from the ode to Eugen, and it appears as though the beauty of these lines should consist in the ambiguity and vagueness of expression:

> Und gleichwohl will das Deutsche Blut
> Den alten Kirchhof feiger Wut
> An neuen Lorbeern fruchtbar machen;
> Und gleichwohl hört der dicke Fluß
> Des Sieges feurigen Entschluß
> Aus Mörsern und Carthaunen krachen.[21]

I will not declare Fleming free of such faults either, particularly in his heroic poetry.[22] Our neighbors the French would find these faults intolerable, having reached the point by virtue of the care devoted to their language where no one is permitted such a vague manner of speech.

Yet these things I have mentioned are not all that one must avoid for the sake of clarity. When one conceals words intended to stir the imagination among a host of superfluous ones, when

---

21   And yet German blood will make
           The old graveyard of cowardly rage
           Fruitful with new laurels;
           And yet the thick flow [of blood] hears
           The fiery resolve of victory
           Roar from mortars and cannon.

These lines, identified by Schlegel as part of the ode to Eugen, are from the second stanza (lines 15–20) of the poem *Auf den zwischen Ihro Kayserlichen Majestät und der Pforte Anno 1718 geschlossenen Frieden* ("To the Peace Concluded Between Your Imperial Majesty and the Pforta [the Turkish Government], 1718").

22 Paul Fleming (1609–1640) was one of the most gifted lyric poets of the German baroque period. More than a third of his writings are in Latin, and even when he writes in his native German he betrays a preference for the forms of classical poetry. However, in complaining of Fleming's faults, especially the "vague manner of speech," Schlegel may have had in mind the poems that were influenced by the dangers and adventures of Fleming's six-year journey to Russia and Persia.

one is too lengthy or too brief at the wrong time, when one uses too many images and leaves the reader no time to observe each feature separately, we also speak of offenses against poetic clarity. The greatest offense in a poem is insipidity, which is nothing more than a lack of those things that make images vivid to our imagination. And, if images are not vivid, how can they be clear? How can a painting be clear if its features are clouded and weak and its colors faded? There would be no end to it if I were to list all the things that aid or harm clarity in each art form, but, because each has its own means for doing that, these rules are more properly intended for those whom the manner and techniques of every art instruct in particular.

19. *If we are to understand fully how pleasure is made intense and order in imitation made fully perceptible, we must also know for whom we are imitating so that we can make use of the temperament of those we desire to please and approach them, as it were, from their most susceptible side.* Imitable things—not all of which are for all people—are so numerous and men's concepts often so opposed to one another that we cannot say exactly for whose sake we should imitate. In order to please the one, we must often disregard the other. Sometimes the model itself will determine for the artist the person to whom the imitation is suitable to afford pleasure. The portrait of a private person is not actually made for everyone, but only for those who know that person. Sometimes the special intent of the artist determines the person to be pleased, without the artist's having been prescribed this by his art. For, if he fulfills the main function of his art, it is a matter of indifference to art to whom it is applied. And so the rule for imitation cannot be more precisely formulated than this: Seek to arouse as much pleasure as your model, the nature of imitation, and those for whom you imitate will allow. *However, if the would-be imitator has no definite intentions in regard to the person for whom he wants to imitate,* the following things can determine to whom he should seek to give pleasure.

If giving pleasure to others is our primary purpose, and if we love all men equally, it is obvious that we want to give *pleasure to as many as possible.* We sometimes find poets who wish to have only a few admirers, not because they actually prefer a few to many, but because most people are so foolish as to make it impossible for them to delight both foolish and clever people at once. Now, it is true that entertaining a clever, understanding person is much more highly regarded than giving pleasure to a fool. But, if we add to the clever person a whole number of less discerning ones, we shall find that we are much more content in having forced, not only the intelligent, but also the most uninitiated, to find pleasure in our work. This is clear evidence of the fact that the pleasure of many is more nearly perfect than the pleasure of only a few. *Nor is it a contradiction to work for both the majority and the clever at the same time,* for, although most people are foolish, we should hardly find as large a number of like-minded fools as of clever people who share the same opinion. Whoever would create for a certain kind of uninitiated person would find all the other unenlightened people against him, because there are many foolish opinions. If, on the other hand, he works for the intelligent, he will have them all on his side. Moreover, he who works in such a way that he must necessarily please everyone unprejudiced in these matters can be certain that posterity will honor him. Horace, who said that a few readers were enough for him,[23] has given pleasure to more people than have other poets of his time who scorned the approval of the whole populace. In this connection, we must make the further distinction that poets who wanted only a few readers were speaking of the approval of experts and not of the pleasure they aroused in clever people.

Approval differs greatly from pleasure. We demand it of only a few connoisseurs, simply because there are only a few connoisseurs. Moreover, their approval is proof to us that we

[23] In one of his *Satires* (I. 10, "An Answer to Critics"), Horace writes: "You must not be concerned for the admiration of the multitude, but must be satisfied with readers who are discriminating but few. . . . It is sufficient for me that the better citizens applaud. I don't care about the rest . . ." (trans. H. W. Wells in *The Complete Works of Horace*, ed. C. J. Kramer, Jr., "Modern Library" [New York: Random House, 1936], p. 39).

are not to blame if we do not manage to afford pleasure to countless people. The great difference between desiring the approbation of many people and wanting to give them pleasure can be seen from this fact: every poet is highly honored as having given pleasure to the fair sex, but he will not boast much of their approval in general and apart from that of individual persons among them. This is true because many such persons cannot know what true and constant pleasure is able to do.

It is evident from the above that whoever imitates something should endeavor to give pleasure to as many as possible, unless he has a special object in mind. *But it is impossible to please everyone because there are too many prejudiced people. Therefore, the surest way to please the greatest number is to try to delight the discerning ones.* The pleasure the imitator thereby creates will be all the more estimable because the discerning person is more deserving of it than the ignorant one. *In respect to art, a discerning person is one who has no prejudices about that art and who possesses a sufficient degree of sensitivity for its works to make an impression on him.* The untrained person of intelligence is as important in this regard as the learned one. And the connoisseur is as worthy of pleasure as a person who does not understand art. The only valid distinction is that made by the vivacity of an unspoiled imagination. *It therefore follows that, in imitating, both original and imitation should be of such a nature—unless the imitator already has other, specific purposes—that they can make a universal impression without presupposing the existence of certain ideas on the part of a particular class of people* and also that they should not be too difficult for people with trained and untrained minds alike, but should serve both at the same time.

20. *Order that we do not perceive cannot afford us pleasure. Yet, we do not perceive the order and similarity of imitation and original if we (whom the representation is supposed to please) have in our minds an idea differing from that of the imitator. In such a case, the pleasure sought cannot be at-*

tained. We see this clearly in classical Greek poetry. Those inadequately acquainted with classical antiquity cannot find pleasure in this poetry, for they either have a concept of ancient heroes and customs different from that of the Greek poets or they do not get the descriptions of these things in their proper intensity, but only in translations, which weaken or distort their characteristics. In our time, we have created a new Achilles, a new Hippolytus—in short, completely new heroes who have a great deal of the nature of great men of our time and are merely put into classical costume. Whoever demands that poems of classical antiquity be identical to our ideas is demanding that the imitation precede the model, for the poems were written several thousand years ago, whereas our ideas did not come to be until modern times. From this I conclude: *whoever imitates must be guided by the ideas of those whom the imitation is intended to please;* that is to say, if their ideas of the original do not correspond to what the original really is, the imitator may no longer take for his model the thing itself, but the ideas of those for whose pleasure he is making the imitation. The latter, then, must be dissimilar to the subject if it is to be more in harmony with the concepts of that subject. One might object that the result would be a spurious pleasure, because the imitation is based on apparent rather than true similarity. Such an objection, however, is easily put aside because the comparison of imitation and original is made in the imagination. The original is therefore not the subject itself, but its concept and image.

Because an imitation is usually only a concept, I should be comparing two totally dissimilar things if I were to liken the concept to the thing itself. If, therefore, the imitation corresponds only to the concept of the original in the minds of those for whose pleasure we imitate, it can never produce an apparent pleasure. For, supposing that the person who has felt this pleasure then changes his idea of the model, he is still constantly aware of the fact that the imitator has yielded to his prejudice and has imitated faithfully, whereas he himself merely had an inaccurate idea from the start.

Although we now have a completely different view of the world from that held in Virgil's and Ovid's time, we still find pleasure in their descriptions. We still delight in reading their depictions of the omnipotence of gods in whom we no longer believe, because we know that they represent perfectly the concepts of their times. But, if a modern poet were to use the same subjects, he would disregard the rules to the same degree that the earlier poets followed them—unless, that is, he took his subjects from such a time and treated them in such a manner that, in thinking of the classical age, we would also unwittingly accept their concepts and believe the poet to be of that age. If the imitator accommodated himself to the ideas of his critics, readers, or spectators (or for whomever he produced his representations), many unjust and premature judgments containing occasional accusations of unnaturalness on the part of the imitator would disappear. For example, who has ever heard a great man speak consistently in the manner of a king or hero of a tragedy? But would we on that account claim that Racine is unnatural because he never wrote a line which does not contain a noble thought? And would we speak of unnaturalness when the host of superfluous words and speeches that inevitably creep into everyday speech (even that of great men) was banished from every tragedy? Or when not a single base word was permitted in tragedy, even though history could prove that a great man had uttered it?

Tragedy imitates the ideas that the majority of people—the more intelligent ones as well—have of great men, especially of dead heroes. Death and time have for the most part taken from these men the things that made them like other people; there is nothing left but those characteristics by which we recognize their superiority over other men. So everyone from childhood on forms a nobler conception of their manner of thinking and speaking than truth demands. Even living heroes avoid social relations to the degree necessary to keep men from getting to know any side which does not show them speaking nobly and of important matters. Tragedy, then, imitates these concepts and can therefore deal only with the connection between noble thoughts and deeds. It is to be praised for this because it not only satisfies our ideas, but also sustains the respect we owe kings.

With this, I believe that I have proved and explained something that seems at first glance utterly false: to imitate well, one must sometimes make the imitation dissimilar to the model.

21. *Things not similar to each other per se can nevertheless attain similarity if we have a concept of one or the other that differs from the true nature of that thing.* In the preceding section, we have been concerned with this possibility insofar as one has a concept of the model that is not identical to it. *This applies also if the imitation is completely dissimilar, not only to the original, but also to the concept one normally has of it. However, such an imitation can still be good if it creates, under certain conditions, an image in our minds similar to the original.*

The first such kind of imitation is optical illusion and anything else that may be termed artistic deception of the senses. In short, I am referring to the things that create a concept in our minds similar to that made by a certain model, not by virtue of their nature, but accidentally; that is, if they are seen in a certain position and from a certain angle or if they are viewed from a certain distance. A tablet on whose narrow, obliquely raised surfaces are painted nothing but indiscernible dots that, when seen from a certain side and at a particular angle, form a complete painting or, as it is customarily called, a *tabula strigata,* is a good and proper imitation. This holds true even if the subject it is supposed to represent does not bear the slightest resemblance to it in terms of that subject's actual composition. To this kind of imitation belongs the theatrical stabbing, in which the dagger seems to penetrate the breast while actually only passing between the arms. But such imitations can be made only when the imitation is truly external and perceived by our senses. They are not possible at all when the representation is formed in our imagination, as is the case with epic poetry, where the representation and the image we have of it in our thoughts are one and the same.

On the other hand, with these latter and with all imitations in general, another faultless imitation can be achieved, namely, that which is not very noticeable and which can be discovered only through most exacting scrutiny. It is often neither possible nor desirable to achieve perfect similarity between objects. But the pleasure aroused in discovering similarities serves to tone down many dissimilarities, if they are well concealed, from the viewer. Also, two things may for that reason seem similar to each other even if many of their features do not correspond, for not everything can be evident in the images that overload, as it were, a person's mind. We see that, because this impression of dissimilarity results from the inattentiveness of others, it cannot be allowed in greater measure than what we would expect to find among the most attentive people. Of course, it remains a deviation from the rule and hence not permissible unless another rule happens to demand it. This is so in order that those who wish to examine the imitation more closely will not notice such a dissimilarity without discovering at the same time a reason to justify it. We see, therefore, that unnoticable dissimilarity does not prevent us from finding things similar even when they are not. A painting is considered similar to its original even when it is viewed from an improper angle. A theater is set up from one angle of vision and yet must be clear to many hundreds of people at the same time. And who can find in poetry two word portraits that are not dissimilar in some way although both may bear a likeness to the person depicted? The Electra of Sophocles, Euripides, Aeschylus, and, among the moderns, Crébillon, are utterly different representations. Yet one cannot say of any one of them that they fail to observe character faithfully. Racine's Achilles is not the Achilles of Corneille, not to mention many other examples that clearly demonstrate the application of our rule and show when it is permissible to make an imitation dissimilar to its model.

22. *A prerequisite for pleasure arising from imitation is the comparison of imitation and original in the minds of those whom the imitation is designed to affect. Consequently, there must be two conceptions in their imagination—one of the original and one of the imitation. If one of these is missing, the entire effect of the imitation will be lost.* This can happen:

(1) *If the imitation is so like its original in all respects that the mind is unable to distinguish them* and considers them the same. I have dealt with this in my essay in defense of verse comedy. In the opinion of some informed friends, there is one objection at least that I ought to raise here: Is such a likeness of imitation and original possible? The philosophical proposition that two things cannot be exactly alike has no bearing here, for they can at least give the appearance of being completely identical. In a comparison of things, the mind pays no attention to slight, imperceptible differences; they are discovered only through exact scrutiny. Moreover, our concepts of the original are indefinite in many details because they are made up of general concepts. Hence, as soon as the mind perceives something that appears to fit the general concept completely, it no longer takes it to be an imitation, but the original. For there is no pleasure to be derived in discovering that a thing is similar to itself! Nor can there be any sense of the pleasure brought about by imitation when I see that one egg is like another or that a tree has the true characteristics of trees.

We find an example of such a natural imitation in faces in which, to the great annoyance of the audience, one cannot distinguish the real from the imitated. A mime, let us say, is supposed to portray a person in great rage. Instead of remaining within the limts of imitated rage and portraying it with understanding, he shows all the characteristics of a genuinely insane person. He is not content merely to rage excessively on the stage; he runs among the audience and carries out his various excesses there, causing the spectators to think that he has become truly mad. And no one in the audience would be grateful to him for this deception.

(2) The second instance in which the main effect of imita-

tion can be lost through lack of an essential concept in the minds of the listeners, spectators, or readers occurs *when these latter have no concept of the model.* A portrait's greatest beauty is lost to all those who do not know the subject and is beautiful only insofar as it bears similarity to a person in general. A poet must therefore know his readers' concepts if his imitation is not to be for naught or, as it were, for another age. The examples and metaphors one used to take from old travel descriptions of Indian fauna and flora—above all anything that had an exotic name—are most unsuitable for imitation. The description of a hen, a female animal,

> Das von dem leichten Volk, so sich in Feldern kleidet,
> Des Kammes kronen gleiche Zier
> Die Wachsamkeit (die Phyllis nie beneidet)
> Und treue Dummheit unterscheidet;
> Das blinden Aberwitz von guten Männern borgt,
> Und Junge fremder Art, als seine Zucht versorgt,[24]

is worth a hundred times more than the depiction of a phoenix, even though in comparison to the phoenix a hen belongs to the plebeians of poultry. The same may also be said of learned descirptions in poems written (in the opinion of their authors), not for the pleasure of the learned, but to delight all classes of people. In the reader's mind, the original is lacking, and therefore the imitations are without force and serve only to annoy him. The most natural description of a pagan god can no longer have the effect today that it had in

[24] The description of a hen is from "Die Henne und der Smaragd" ("The Hen and the Emerald"), one of the *Fabeln und Erzählungen* ("Fables and Tales") of Friedrich von Hagedorn. The 1757 edition of the collected works offers a variant reading of the fifth line: "Das blinde Gütigkeit . . ." instead of "Das blinden Aberwitz . . . ," i.e., "which blind benevolence" instead of the dubious and altogether inappropriate "which blind conceit."

> Which is distinguished from the flighty folk who clad
>   themselves in feathers
> By the crownlike ornament of the comb,
> By vigilance (Phyllis never envied this),
> And by faithful stupidity;
> Which borrows blind benevolence from good men
> And cares for the young of a brood other than its own.

Virgil's time; it seems to have been made only for lovers of antiquity. To a person without learning, the description,

> Wenn holdes Weigern, sanftes Zwingen,
> Verliebter Diebstahl, reizend Singen,
> Mit Wollust beyder Herz beräuscht;
> Wenn der verwirrte Blick der Schönen,
> Ihr schwimmend Aug voll seichter Thränen
> Was sie verweigert, heimlich heischt,[25]

will be much more charming than Venus' girdle and the description Homer gives of it.

But from this we cannot conclude that things our readers have not actually seen ought not to be imitated. If they are familiar only with the parts of a thing, they will be able to construct it in their minds. Nor can it be concluded that we may not describe a new and hitherto-unknown species of something; on the contrary, the reader's pleasure is infinitely heightened when we acquaint him with something new— either in nature or in the realm of representations—by showing him a copy or imitation of it. We also increase his knowledge thereby, especially if the strange, unknown things have something wondrous and attractive about them.

From this it follows that we should either choose subjects to imitate that are already part of the concepts of those we are attempting to please, or, in those cases where we have reason to imitate unknown things, we should seek ways and means to give a concept of the original along with its representation. At this moment, three such means occur to me as particularly useful in poetry—whereby I do not mean to deny that there can be others as well. One is to give a description of something along with its representation as an aid to forming a concept of it. An example of this is to characterize the person whose

---

[25] When charming refusal, gentle forcing,
amorous theft, delightful struggling
enrapture both hearts in bliss;
when the disconcerted glance of the fair maiden,
her moist eyes filled with insipid tears,
secretly demands what she declines,

Schlegel fails to identify these lines, presumably by a contemporary or late-seventeenth-century German poet.

actions one is imitating. If we check this in poetic descriptions, we often find a slight addition to the name of the object described which identifies it in some way. True, this addition, often an adjective or a brief paraphrase, is sometimes a part of the depiction itself. But occasionally it is for the purpose of giving the reader a notion of a strange subject so that the depiction to follow can please him all the more.

Another means of offering him a concept of the model of something unfamiliar is to give a description by parts in such a way that the person seeing or hearing it is reminded of a part of the original and thus learns to construct the unfamiliar subject from familiar parts. Someone with no concept (*Vorstellung*) of the Sphinx can still derive pleasure from a description in which all its parts are designated and thus depicted.

Finally, the third means of offering a concept (*Begriff*) of an unfamiliar subject is by comparison, or simile. This is a substitute for the model and is more pleasant because it gives a representation of a completely different object, as well as a model or copy of the object in question. As a result, we perceive twice as much order and have twice as much pleasure simply because there are double representations.

(3) One would not suppose that *an imitator could neglect to awaken in his reader a concept of the imitation*. And yet this happens in all inferior poems in which only the names of things are given, rather than descriptions. Names give the reader merely the model, and, if the reader thinks that he is going to get its imitation or image, he is mistaken. If I say that a frog croaks, I am not yet imitating the frog. But we find poems in which everything that is said comes out just this way and in which we see no more images than in the words I am writing here. This lack of images can never come about, however, if one attempts to put into a work that which I spoke of in the first part of this essay, where I attempted to explain the nature of poetic imitation.

23. The proposition that *a strong emotion suppresses a weaker one* is propounded by psychology and accepted everywhere as a fact. Accordingly, order arising from imitation can-

not be perceived if at the same time something else exerts a stronger influence on the imagination for which one imitates. Emotions that are aroused by something other than the process of imitation and its product (which is intended to please) and that divert the mind from a contemplation of the representation cannot be affected by imitation. Indeed, we must regard emotions that destroy the primary purpose of imitation as matters of chance, which we can neither foresee nor change. We cannot be surprised that a person filled with sadness and consternation passes through a gallery of beautiful paintings without seeing them, let alone examining their obvious features. *But an imitator would work against himself if his representations stirred up such strong emotions that the feeling for the beauty of the imitation were either weakened or utterly suppressed.*

One might object that imitation cannot possibly arouse an emotion capable of suppressing the pleasure it gives. What is seen in the mind's eye can never create as strong an impression as what is perceived in reality. Except for pleasure, the emotions aroused by an imitation are not actual feelings of sadness or terror or disgust, but are only their concepts and can therefore never be so strong as these passions themselves. Consequently, we may say that they cannot be so powerful as to suffocate the true feeling of pleasure aroused by the imitation. It is true that the pleasure we take in similarity is, for the most part, the only true emotion created by the imitation and that almost all other emotions that it creates are nothing more than extremely vivid fancies. Despite this fact, however, such a vivid conception can outweigh a none-too-captivating object. The misfortunes of another do not move us as deeply as our own; but, on the other hand, someone else's great misfortune can move us more deeply than a small loss we ourselves have suffered. In many imitations, if they affect the imagination through sense impressions, there is, in addition to the pleasure derived from imitation, something that awakens true passions and not mere mental impressions. Aeschylus' furies, as they were seen in the theater, inspired such great terror because they appealed to the senses and truly stirred them.

There are also emotions in regard to which we are by no means so certain that a mental concept is weaker than a mental impression of the same object. The mental image sometimes permits us to analyze carefully an object from which we would turn our eyes if we saw it in reality. Disgust seems to me to be an example of this. It is a sensation aroused far more by describing a disgusting object in detail than by looking at it. And I confess that I would rather see an ugly old woman than read a detailed description of her. Hence, if we are to avoid this error and deserve the thanks of those for whom we imitate when we awaken unpleasant rather than pleasant sensations in them, we must consider how strong an impression each kind of imitation makes, both in regard to the impression of similarity and to the other sensations it awakens, and see to it that the impression of similarity is stronger than the others.

Each kind of imitation has its particular effects in this respect. A painter may depict more disgusting objects than a poet, because an exact description of something disgusting is far more unpleasant than a vicarious viewing of it. One may imitate more terrible things in epic works than in theatrical presentations.

If, after examining all this, we find that a certain subject possesses qualities that would create an unpleasant and a stronger impression than that which we have when we perceive similarity, we may resort to one of two means to avoid such an error. We may simply give up the subject; or, if there are so many beautiful things bound up with it that it would be a pity not to imitate it, we may conceal anything that could cause these incompatible impressions. In our imitation, we should weaken their effect and preferably depict the subject somewhat less vividly and naturally, rather than lose the entire value of the imitation through exaggerated fidelity. It would strike the spectator as an offense against propriety and hence annoy him if we were to show Venus or the naked Americans [Indians] on the stage or in the kind of clothing that would make them seem naked. But, before we give up, on that account, these characters and all the impressions of beauty that they can awaken in our minds, it is better to give them clothing as little different as possible from what they are accustomed to wearing and to have our pleasure in seeing them. Better, I say, than to be annoyed at them for appearing unclad, as nature would demand. If one saw the convulsions of a dying man and the frothing of a madman on the stage, the effect would be one of horror. Thus, it is better to choose the tolerable aspects of these two and present death without horror and insanity without loathsomeness than to expose oneself to such abomination and to rob oneself of the pleasure to be found in good imitations of these subjects.

24. *When the order that is created by imitation and brought about by the similarity between representation and model is combined with other perfect features of the representation without loss of similarity, the result is a greater degree of pleasure than that which is aroused by similarity alone. But, since pleasure is the chief aim for imitation it is advisable to seek to further this aim by secondary as well as the principal means and to increase the intended pleasure in every way possible.*

The rules just given are not necessary to imitation, but are arbitrary; however, in most of the arts they are, on careful consideration, combined with imitation. *The secondary means of increasing pleasure are present either in the model and its characteristics or in the medium of the imitation. If the characteristics of the model are themselves very pleasant and possess a high degree of order, this order is carried over into the model itself.* One can readily imagine that it is more pleasant to draw a likeness of a splendid palace than to paint a plain, square table. The order inherent in the original is of such a quality that it can never dull the beauty of the imitation, but must enhance it. In an object possessing inherent order, the uniformity of parts is all the more visible; and the more evident this uniformity, the more readily one can perceive the similarities between imitation and model. It is much easier to err in the attempt to produce similarity if the subject is a wild region in which no part or feature stands in harmonious relation to another than if the subject is a palace whose every part is measured. I do not mean to imply that a wild region has no other beauties to justify its being imitated; I am only mentioning this to explain one particular perfect feature of a model.

In short, the better the model's order, the more perfect features it will possess and the more suitable it will be for imitating—if, that is to say, all its other aspects are harmonious, if the medium is well suited to take on a similarity to the model, and if the imitator is up to the task. One of the greatest of a model's perfect features, especially if the model is more evident to the mind than to the senses, is its ability to instruct. Nothing gives a man's mind more pleasure than to be taught, particularly if the imitation does not give the impression of teaching. All those who give the appearance of resisting any form of instruction are not resisting instruction and the joy of learning something themselves, but the apparent fact that they did not know something and had to learn it from someone else. But their pleasure is considerable if they can increase their knowledge under the guise of doing something else.

Consequently, the most pleasant models are the most instructive. Besides, we always have a much clearer notion of an instructive thing (as something most deserving of our attention) than we do of trivialities. As a result, we can also grasp similarity from the imitation of such a subject.

Finally, it is a subject in which our good sense tells us to combine so worthy a secondary purpose with its pleasant primary aim, since both can be attained simultaneously and be of mutual advantage. We need have no fear, therefore, that, in the attempt to choose always the highest degree of perfection, the same model will be hit upon. The greatest degree of perfection in two separate cases involving models of one kind is most rare, because in every imitation there are secondary aims that always dictate the choice of one model over the others.

If I were to list here all the rules governing the choice of a model, I would not only need a separate section, but I would also digress from the general line of my treatise and find it necessary to investigate separately the models of each art. Furthermore, I would be doing something superfluous for poetry, because there are already sufficiently detailed treatises on the choice of a medium, the art of endowing the medium with more dignity and splendor, the element of the miraculous in a poem's contents, and such things. *This kind of arbitrary order and perfection, with which one combines the necessary order created by the imitation, can be present also in the medium of the imitation. Sometimes it can also help to make clearer the order produced by similarity; sometimes it has no such effect.* What we call poetic style in poetry is of the first sort. It is possible to give a description of something without using words borrowed from other things and used on this occasion for purposes of comparison. I believe that the verses by Professor Gottsched that I have already quoted are of this kind.

> Schaue, wie sich Haupt und Glied
> Fleisch und Bein so künstlich fügen,
> Wie sich Flächs und Sähne zieht,
> Wie die vollen Muskeln liegen.
> Gieb auf deiner Adern Menge
> Und des Blutes Kreislauf acht,
> Den das Herz mit reger Macht,
> Durch sein spritzendes Gedränge,
> In die kleinsten Zäsern treibt,
> Daß kein Pünktchen saftlos bleibt.[26]

If the model possesses a high degree of perfection, it needs the assistance of figurative language least of all. But, if one wanted to give a description in one's own words either longer than this or not about such perfect things, the results would

---

[26] See above, p. 20, note 8.

be pale and lifeless. I cannot explain more fully here the advantages that such a style has for imitation, because this has already been done adequately by many classical and modern writers and because this aspect of poetry has often been confused with the true nature of poetry. Everything said of conceits and similes belongs to this embellishment of poetic imitation insofar as they are used in epic description. I want to state only the following here: Just as the arbitrary embellishments of imitation make the representations livelier when used prudently, so do certain of these embellishments, if used too often, becloud the imitations and cause us to forget in our constant examination of these incidental beauties the imitations themselves and their similarity to the originals. We are thus led away from the primary aim and into seemingly pleasant byways.

These are, in brief form, my thoughts on poetic style. They cannot be treated fully in a treatise on imitation, but demand a separate work in itself—which I need not undertake, however, since poetic style is the best and most frequently treated of all aspects of poetry. Nonetheless, in all that I have ever said on this subject, one will find nothing to justify the accusation made against me that I would censure a poet for unprecedented expressions. In my opinion, one should never judge that an expression is too daring, because not audacity, novelty, or anything else except inaccuracy of expression can be culpable. And such culpability occurs when the expression is improper in itself or with respect to the character of the person uttering it. Instead of taking refuge behind the obscure words "daring" and "unheard of," one ought to seek the reasons for the inaccuracies. This could decide the matter once and for all. Besides, the term "unheard of" is extremely ambiguous. In everyday speech, one says "That is unheard of!" if one is trying to indicate that something is excessive or so odd that one would never have thought to hear such as that. But in a more lofty style this word is used for something which has never been heard before and is new and wonderful. I am citing this in the hope that the term will be used more carefully in order that one may at least avoid misunderstanding in the disputes that have arisen over the unprecedented or excessive in poetic style.

Meter in poetry is likewise a perfect feature connected to the furtherance of pleasure in imitation. The early practitioners of poetry have identified this arbitrary device so intimately with poetry that one renounces the nature of poetry and invents a new kind of imitation if meter is taken away. I have no doubt that another will find more to say than I if he knows how to imitate nature in music, painting, dramatic art, and the other arts, of which I can boast no special knowledge. But it was my desire to communicate to others at least my thoughts on this subject and to leave it to them to improve or make use of what I have discussed here.

Letter to N. N. Concerning Verse Comedy

SIR:

Certain gentlemen have now settled on the opinion that a comedy should be written in prose, and they have openly formed a society whose head lends by his approval even more weight to their claims.[1] Although one can surmise that they must have had serious reasons for forming a judgment on which they had reflected for so long, I feel that it would be wrong of me merely to refute their opinion without at the same time proving the opposite. The case for verse comedy is not so weak that one must content oneself with rejecting the accusations made against it without being able to prove its superiority to prose comedy. Moreover, one would be forever in doubt as to whether a true case against the opponents of verse comedy had been made. As a result, verse comedy could not be covered against all attacks, but only against those of the aforementioned gentlemen and, what is more, against only the particular attack that they have dared to make. Meanwhile, I cannot refrain from raising an objection which seems to be so important a proof that it is used, not only by these particular opponents of verse comedy, but by everyone who has anything against this form. Afterward, I shall show that verse comedy is preferable to prose comedy. And, finally, since the question as to whether a comedy should be in verse is not the same as asking whether we Germans adopt appropriate verse for comedy, I shall endeavor to convince my opponents that our rhymed verse is just as suitable to comedy as to other kinds of poetry.

The most impressive argument against verse comedy is that

[1] The "certain gentlemen" referred to are Gottsched and Straube; the approving head is, of course, Gottsched himself. See Introduction, pp. xxii–xxiii.

people who ought to give the appearance of speaking spontaneously talk in verse and that this is not only improbable but impossible.

All arts that aim at imitating nature select a certain medium in which to carry out their imitation. For example, a sculptor chooses to imitate nature in stone or wood; painters select a flat surface on which the things to be viewed are depicted in the arrangement and manner in which we actually see them. Some painters even aim at rendering their pictures in the same colors we see in the objects themselves. Others are content merely to denote light and shadow. Yet, one cannot for that reason say that any of them performed improperly. Music and poetry, finally, attempt, each in its own way, to form an image of nature by means of harmonious sounds. No one is obliged to imitate an object in all its qualities and to give the copy all possible points of similarity with the original, for in such a case there could be only one true imitation of any object. Moreover, the imitation would not be merely similar to the original; it would be completely identical to it. If the gentlemen wanted to claim that an imitation must be similar in all respects to its model, they would not be able to acquiesce in the banishment of verse from comedy but, by the same token, would have to grant the strong unlikelihood that people—for example, maids in comedy, who certainly had no language teachers—would speak the language as correctly and purely as though they had been trained. For, after all, a poet surely ought not to let his characters make grammatical errors without important cause or unless he needs to ridicule something he had threaded into his work.

However, they could counter me by citing Molière's Swiss.[2] And so I shall list for them a number of things improbable in comedy and yet required by its rules. For example, is it not just as improbable for one single action to occur in a single

[2] In order to hoodwink the parents, the scoundrel Scapin (in Molière's *Les Fourberies de Scapin* ["That Scoundrel Scapin"], 1671) is beset by imaginary enemies, whose voices are those of Scapin himself. The assumed accents are Gascon and Swiss (Act III).

place without being interrupted by other actions, which in everyday life so often interrupt our affairs? Or for all the characters to appear at just the time and point in the dialogue when we want them—something utterly impossible if we are to speak of external reality? And so we must concede that, in all imitations of nature, one can determine how and to what extent one wants to imitate. Granted that a poet disregards nature in this respect and has his characters speak in verse, he is no more to be criticized than a painter ought to be reproached for making a pen-and-ink drawing of something and thus not giving it the colors it possesses in reality or that a sculptor should be expected to color the statue he intends to carve from stone and leave white or to cover his animal sculpture with fur. If I wanted to go further, I could say that meter is actually the medium in which the poet imitates and portrays nature. And I could say that he who imitates nature in prose in the manner in which poets have presumed to imitate and who has many things in common with a poet does not deserve that name in any real sense because he lacks an essential ingredient of poetry, namely, the harmonious sound of meter.

But, in order not to become involved in other quarrels, I shall content myself with having shown that, in imitating nature, it is permissible to choose the manner and medium of imitation and that anyone who fails to imitate in certain respects is not for that reason imitating poorly. Consequently, a comedy cannot be called faulty for being in verse, although we should still have the choice of charging verse or prose with the office of providing pleasure through comedy. Even though poetry has existed for a long time and has laid claim to comedy from the very beginning, I venture to say that, if we had had only prose comedies for the same length of time, we would now begin to write them in verse. However, since we have inherited comedy in verse from Greece and Rome, I need only justify the taste of these peoples—which has been so delicate in such things—and show that it is not caprice but reason or the greater pleasure that attached comedy to poetry.

Since the pleasure derived from the imitation is the ultimate purpose of imitating nature, imitation misses its purpose when pleasure ceases. All sensory pleasure arises from order. Thus, when the imitation pleases, it does so by virtue of a sense of order as well. Things which of themselves have no similarity in structure can awaken pleasure when they are imitated. As I see it, pleasure is brought about in the following way: Imitation consists in the similarity between copy and original, and this similarity lies in the fact that the parts of the one stand in the same relation to one another as do the parts of the other. I believe that I am at liberty to speak mathematically.[3] Let us assume parts A, B, and C of the original, and, lest the order arising from the similarity of original and copy be confused with the order that the parts of the one may have among themselves, I shall further assume that the parts A, B, and C of the original have no similar relation among themselves. The parts of the copy we shall call D, E, and F, and part D of the copy will correspond to part A of the original, and part E, to part B. The copy will thus be similar to the original when D is to E as A to B and F to C. In this way, similar relations will hold between A and D, B and E, and C and F. And, though the parts of the original have no similar relations whatever, a high degree of similarity—and thereby much pleasure—will arise from mere imitation if I place original and copy side by side. Yet, this pleasure vanishes as soon as one removes the original and looks only at the copy, for, since A, B, and C

---

[3] Two writings in particular may be cited as influential in Schlegel's use of mathematical method and analysis: Christian Wolff's (1679-1754) *Der Anfangs-Gründe aller mathematischen Wissenschaften Erster Teil* ("First Principles of the Science of Mathematics, Part I," 1710), and *Vernünfftige Gedanken von den Kräften des menschlichen Verstandes und ihrem richtigen Gebrauch in Erkänntnis der Wahrheit* ("Sensible Thoughts on the Powers of the Human Intellect and Their Proper Use in the Perception of Truth," 1738). The opening section of the first treatise, "Kurze Unterricht von der mathematischen Lehrart" ("Short Lessons in Mathematical Theory"), appears to have formed the basis for Schlegel's reasoning in this section of the verse-comedy essay. (See Antoniewicz, pp. xxxii ff.)

have no similar relations to one another, D, E, and F will likewise have none if I regard them independently and without considering the parts of the original.

This loss of pleasure will occur when similar relations among the parts of the copy no longer hold, namely, when A:D, likewise B:E and C:F. For in this manner the imitation is not merely similar to the original, but identical to it; and in our minds we confuse the two, since there is nothing in the imitation itself to remind us that it is not the original, but a copy, that we have before us. Consequently, all the pleasure that can be derived from an imitation vanishes. If, for example, we are led into a forest that art has made so similar to a real forest as to be indistinguishable from it, no pleasure whatever is felt beyond that which a real forest affords because we take it to be real. If we were finally told that the forest had been created by art, we would admire the skill of its creator but would soon again confuse the natural forest with the manufactured one. The result would be that we would feel the pleasure given us by something in which art, as it were, gleams forth from behind the similarity of imitation to original and thus enables us to compare constantly original and copy without ever confusing them.

It is a hard and fast rule that one should never make imitations so completely similar to their models that they do not differ from them in any perceptible way. And I can show with as many examples as there are imitative arts that this rule is grounded in experience. To cite merely one or the other example, we customarily make a grotto to resemble the caves in which, as some say, man lived long ago, before he learned to build houses and towns. Would one look with so much pleasure at the presentation at court of farm life if the ladies were dressed in homespuns and in their outward appearance offered nothing by which we could distinguish them from true peasant women? Our pleasure in such a scene is due to the fact that the presentation is similar to but more beautiful than a farm.

By the same token, prose comedy has as little right to pride itself on the fact that it is not merely natural, but nature itself.

But what does comedy have, except for verse, that one constantly associates with it and all its parts and that everywhere distinguishes it from a real-life conversation yet does not utterly destroy its similarity to life? If one were to say that we know it to be a comedy and not a real event anyway, one would be citing a characteristic extrinsic to comedy. Moreover, we should thank the author for writing it in such a way that we do not need to reflect on it or perhaps take the figures portrayed to be the real people they are meant to represent. To build real houses on the stage would not be nearly so perfect an imitation as that obtained by means of mere painted props. And, if I recall correctly, the English *Spectator,* in speaking of the songbirds of the opera, has said various things relevant to our subject.[4]

But, granted that one could find something other than verse that would be related to all parts of comedy and everywhere distinguish imitation from original, I intended to say that at least one could find nothing better for this purpose.

Often, when we want to distinguish a copy from its original, we leave out some point of similarity (as I illustrated above

[4] In the fifth number of *The Spectator* (March 6, 1711), Addison asserts that "an opera may be allowed to be extravagantly lavish in its Decorations, as its only Design is to gratifie the Senses, and keep up an indolent Attention in the Audience." In regard to naturalism, Addison favors resemblances, not the things themselves: "A little Skill in Criticism would inform us, that Shadows and Realities ought not to be mix'd together in the same Piece; and that Scenes, which are designed as the Representations of Nature, should be filled with Resemblances, and not with the Things themselves." Addison's illustration of this plea for the imaginary rather than the real concerns real sparrows, which were "to enter towards the end of the first Act, and to fly about the Stage." The sparrows, Addison says, were "to act the part of Singing Birds in a delightful Grove." His disapproval of such a practice is not restricted merely to theoretical considerations: "But to return to the Sparrows: there have been so many Flights of them let loose in this Opera, that it is feared the House will never get rid of them; and that in other Plays they may make their Entrance in very wrong and improper Scenes, so as to be seen flying in a Lady's Bed-Chamber, or pearching upon a King's Throne; besides the Inconveniences which the Heads of the Audience may sometimes suffer from them."

with the uncolored sculpture) and isolate some aspect of the original, as for example here the figure, which we take over into the copy. But comedy, by virtue of verse, is able to make a distinction between what it copies and the copy itself without leaving out anything. Comedy imitates the actions of men in everyday life in all details; but, whereas in its presentation actions, customs, speech, dress, manners, and voice coincide fully with real-life action, the varied harmonious sounds and the regularly structured relation of syllables to one another distinguish it from true action. Meter, being nonessential to words, does not by any means prevent them from corresponding exactly to the probable thoughts of the person expressing them. And all words in comedy can have the highest probability insofar as this probability lies, not in the relation of words to one another, but in their appropriateness to the thoughts and in the probability of the things they are meant to express. Verse comedy is thus distinguished from real action in that it creates with the highest possible degree of similarity to real action a new kind of order, namely, the harmony of syllables. Now, it must be conceded that a thing is the more nearly perfect the more perfections it brings together without conflict with one another. But, since verse itself does not prevent similarity of imitated action to real or suppress any of the correspondences it has to real action, verse comedy is to be preferred to prose. This is true also because it possesses, in addition to other perfections, one more than prose.

All ideas are given greater emphasis and a much more perceptible charm when the harmony of meter is added to their own natural merit. And they increase not only the spectator's pleasure; by impressing themselves on his memory through their charm and the ease with which they can be remembered, they extend over many days the pleasure given by a single performance. And, because they often stir about within our minds, they reawaken the same feeling we had during the performance of the play. The ancients loved nothing better than citing verse, especially that taken from plays; and one has been able to find a considerable number of lines from Menander's comedies in the works of other writers who quoted him. Still, this is not the only perfection verse comedy has that prose does not.

We feel no slight degree of pleasure when we are constantly led, not only by the similarity of copy to original, but by the copy itself to the art of its makers. In this way, the concept of perfection in those who created the pleasure is joined to our pleasure in the thing itself. And it is precisely this which a comedy does better in verse than in prose. The author of a prose comedy seems to us to be no more than a historian, and we perceive no difference between his scenes and a real-life conversation. But every line of a well-written verse comedy gives us insights into the poet's art, as well as into the similarity of comedy to natural actions. All words in comedy have the same natural connection to one another that they would also have without meter, and they flow from the speaker's mouth so effortlessly that one might think that these people could not speak differently in real life. At the same time, all the syllables are in harmonious relation to one another. And, if the words themselves entice us into believing that we are listening to natural speech, their euphony reminds our ears that it is a work of art, and we are suddenly presented for our greater pleasure with a true action, its imitation, and the artistry of its creator. Indeed, if I regard the individual speeches of characters in comedy rather than the organization of the whole, I reach the conclusion that, once the edifice (or, better, skeleton) of a comedy is achieved, little art is required to write a comedy without verse. To put the proper words into the mouths of the kind of persons I see and hear daily does not require a great deal of reflection; and, once the characters are decided on, little more is needed than to set down from memory the speech of such people. Indeed, experience teaches us that the actors themselves—and that includes those with little knowledge—are quite adept at doing this. When they are given the subject of the comedy and know the scene sequence, they will soon find the dialogue. And, it seems to me, we have no cause to complain that the figures we encounter in everyday life do not use appropriate speech. In fact, I find that their speech is more natural than we would demand in the name of honesty. However, if the poet chooses words that can be put into a certain meter without losing their naturalness or violating even slightly the nature of the person to be portrayed, it must be said that he displays his art and skill in every word.

Plays in verse enhance the actor's as well as the poet's art. I do not deny that there is an art to endowing prose with the tone that a person of this or that temperament would use. But it will be granted me, in turn, that it is a far greater art to do this in verse. A not unimportant reason for going to a play, which we would otherwise be able to read at home, is to see the art with which it is performed. And so we appreciate verse comedy also because it reveals such great differences in performance and distinguishes a good actor from a mediocre one.

These, then, are the proofs that in my reflections on the nature of pleasure and perfection have convinced me—and give me no slight hope of convincing the gentlemen—that verse comedy is not only not self-contradictory, but far preferable to prose comedy. To this I shall add only the following.

What we have been able to say about the nature of pleasure was necessarily derived from our experience; that is, we observed the actual cause of this or that unpleasant sensation. We can thus judge the beauty of a thing from the amount of pleasure it gives to most people who have either given free rein to their minds, so to say, and not let them become artificial and oversophisticated by unnatural thinking or who have improved them in a fitting way. And we can do this just as reliably as we can by means of rules. This is especially true when we consider that the approval a thing earns is preserved for an extended period among various civilized nations. Yet, we observe that, from the very beginning, verse comedy was written by the Greeks, taken over by the Romans (likewise in verse), and gradually restored to its right by the French after the actors' ignorance had caused it to be abandoned in favor of prose during a time when the poor state and barbaric age of comedy prevailed. Finally, as Monsieur Voltaire says in his preface to *Brutus,* even Molière's comedies, which were in prose, had to be recast in verse after his death.[5] As for the Italians, it is no wonder that verse has not yet been fully introduced, considering the poor state in which one usually finds their comedy. Because the actors appear on stage without knowing what lines they are to speak and therefore have to improvise, it is easy to see the reason for their comedies' usually (though not always) having no verse. The English, likewise, have nothing valid to show in this respect. Their comedies are not what one could properly call comedies because for the most part they are more a mixture of many separate plots and a stringing together of a number of characters than real comedies, written with a definite end in mind. And so one finds that the English have not yet devoted enough attention to comedy to bring about its improvement. And this, too, can easily have escaped the gentlemen's attention.

To be sure, they wanted to answer these objections in advance; and so, to extricate themselves from the situation, they hit on the unheard-of notion of saying that a comedy must be in verse in order to aid the actor's memory. But would anyone nowadays work so many months longer than one had to just to spare an actor at most one additional day's effort? And, what is more, to produce something about which one knew that, in the actor's opinion, it would have been better to save oneself the trouble! Elsewhere, perhaps, actors had a different sort of memory from that of our actors. It cannot be denied that rhyme makes our verse far easier than classical verse to

[5] In his *Discours sur la tragédie* [*Brutus*], Voltaire makes the claim that rhyme is not only necessary to French tragedy, but also embellishes its comedies, "mais elle embellit nos comédies mêmes," and he concludes his brief argument with the words: "en un mot, nous avons des comédies en prose du célèbre Molière, que l'on a été obligé de mettre en vers après sa mort, et qui ne sont plus jouées que de cette manière nouvelle" ("In a word, we have comedies in prose by the celebrated Molière that had to be put into verse after his death and are no longer performed in any other but this new manner") *Œuvres complètes de Voltaire* (Paris, 1828), I, 371–372.

learn. Yet, how many actors there are whose principal objection to performing verse comedy is that they cannot learn it!

They know, finally, that the first dramatists performed their own plays and, what is more, at a time when plays were simple and no doubt gave the impression of being almost exclusively monologues. Because it was only later thought to be a tremendous improvement when two persons conversed, the author usually recited the whole play himself. Thus, if he wrote in verse merely because he could learn it by heart, why did it not occur to Demosthenes or some other orator who likewise had much to recite from memory to write his speech in verse and thereby save himself effort in memorizing—especially since in their opinion iambic verse was not heard as such and it therefore could not have mattered to the audience whether a speech was in prose or iambic verse meter?

But, they will say, it would be unfair not to reckon the Germans among those whose judgments carry weight. For all that, many people—among them, important persons and particularly those familiar with criticism—do not delight in a performance of our verse comedies, but find a prose comedy more natural. For my part, I believe that most of these people have not based their opinion on their own feelings, but on various and rather obvious reasons, and I think that such people react to verse comedy much like those who submit a proposition to the sort of experiments one makes in science. For, just as they let themselves be readily persuaded that they have observed in the experiment itself what they already postulated, so, too, have those who were prejudiced against verse judged less according to their feelings than to the rule they made for themselves. I have been assured of this in great part by these same people, and I remember quite well their confessing to me that they wished it were appropriate to write verse comedy, because they enjoyed it and only feared that their pleasure was part of the great love they had for verse in general. Up to this moment—and as long as they continue to have this pleasure—I am unable to take their objections to verse comedy as anything more than critical compunctions. For my part, and despite the fact that I do not venture to place my feelings in opposition to those of such noteworthy people as they have on their side, I can state that I have seen a performance of Voltaire's *Prodigal Son* in translation; [6] and this is the only verse comedy I have seen performed. Whenever I noticed a particularly lively passage or a tone that struck truer to nature—as was not seldom the case—I surely felt as much pleasure as I did on seeing an equally vigorous performance of a prose play.

We have not yet brought ourselves to accept unrhymed verse on our stage. And, although those who ventured to write such verse deserve the gratitude of all Germans for having tried to secure for our literature the advantage once enjoyed by the Greeks and Romans (especially since they thereby taught us to heed, not only the formal aspects of verse, but also the veritable beauty residing in the thoughts), we Germans have until now been so obstinate that we preferred to demand that poets be guided by what our ears were accustomed to hearing rather than to attempt to accustom our ears to this new kind of verse. We have therefore begun to use rhymed six-foot iambs in our comedies. That this form is not unsuitable to comedy is the final point I have promised to demonstrate.

In the first place, I do not need to answer the gentlemen when they say that it is improbable for a person to rhyme his

[6] Voltaire's *L'Enfant prodigue, Comédie en cinq actes*, was first produced on October 10, 1736. Two German translations existed in Schlegel's time, both, according to Straube, equally poor. See W. M. A. Creizenach (*Zur Entstehungsgeschichte des neueren deutschen Lustspiels* [Halle: 1879], pp. 38–39): "Voltaire's *Enfant prodigue* wurde sehr bald nach seinem Erscheinen (1737) in Deutschland eingebürgert; Koch übersetzte es. . . . Noch vor der Koch'schen Übersetzung wurde eine andere in Leipzig aufgeführt, gleichfalls in Versen" ("Voltaire's *Prodigal Son* was brought into Germany soon after its publication; Koch translated it. . . . Even before the Koch translation, another one, likewise in verse, was performed in Leipzig"). This earlier translation, Creizenach speculates, was done by a certain Uhlich, secretary to the Neuber theater troupe.

words with another's or, indeed, that a person often arrives at this rhyme only after the rhyme-word of the preceding verse has already been uttered (and yet he is in effect rhyming with a verse he had not yet heard!). I can only repeat what I have already said: It is by no means necessary to look for probability in the sound of the verses, but rather in the medium in which the poet is attempting to imitate nature. The probability of words consists in their appropriateness to the thoughts they express, not in the external relationship of the sounds of the words to one another. But, if one says that, because rhyme demands words of a certain sound, it forces us to employ words not corresponding fully to our thoughts, then I confess that there is a good deal of illusion in the matter. For sound dictates to me the letters that the word occurring in this place is supposed to have. But how can I always find words with the required letters and, beyond that, the required meaning? If this is true, it is a fault of all German poetry and not of comedy alone. But, even if I allowed that our poetry had this major fault of forcing us to use words and then to seek a meaning for them, experience and the example of so many great men who have written in our language would prevent me from granting this. I hope that the gentlemen will not say that these writers were forced by rhyme to say what they did not think; the good logic of their thoughts shows that we do injustice to rhyme.

In our contemporary poetry, rhyme has the effect of making our verse forms somewhat ponderous. Considering the light and graceful quality of our meter, this is, in my opinion, a good thing in that it causes us to pause a moment at each verse, thus affording us the opportunity to select our expression and weigh our choice of words more carefully. In this way, our thoughts become more polished and, wherever it is required, our manner of expression livelier and more elegant.

But if we insist nevertheless on regarding rhyme as a relic of the bards, I should almost believe that it was provided for at the very outset by the structure of our poetry, and I should believe that rhyme would always be indispensable in the kind of caesura found in our six-foot iambic verse. As soon as we omit rhyme from the caesura, we appear to divide every line into two short verses. The caesura thus has nothing to distinguish it from the verse end; and since one part of the verse has the same number of feet as the other, I have the impression of always hearing three-foot iambs. If we sought to avoid this by using feminine end rhymes for all verses, we should find such poetry unbearable. Indeed, we cannot even endure two successive verses with feminine endings that do not rhyme. Both the Italians and the English use five-foot iambs for their unrhymed verse, the former with feminine and the latter with masculine end rhymes only. But our ears are too sensitive for the first, and our language too unmusical for the latter. In fact, it appears that we could not endure one long poem written in this kind of verse.

A learned professor of the academy here [7] holds the view that it would be better if those who first used our verse had put the caesura after the third foot, in the manner of the Greeks and Romans. It cannot be denied that both Romans and Greeks employed the caesura in their iambic verse—in comedy, too—although the Latin comedy writers, and especially Plautus (the Romans did not yet have the refined ear of the age of Augustus), did not do so with the precision of the Greeks. To cite the first line of Plautus:

Ut vos in vostris / voltis mercimoniis [8]

Here the caesura is, I think, rather evident. But, just as in their heroic verse the Romans permitted themselves the freedom of placing the caesura after the fourth foot, so did Plautus in his iambic verse. In Aristophanes' iambs, the caesura is exactly placed:

[7] The learned professor was Johann Friedrich Christ (1700–1756), who held the chair for poetry at Leipzig during Schlegel's stay there and who probably exerted considerable influence on the young dramatist.

[8] In Plautus' *Amphitruo*, Mercury, disguised as Sonia, begins the "Prologue" with these words: "As you wish in your business [that I help you, so you listen to this play]."

ὡς ἀργαλέον πρᾶγμ' / ἔστιν ὦ γῆ χαὶ θεοί.[9]

And, with the exception of the twelfth line of *Plutus*, they will not find a single verse in which the caesura falls at the end of the fourth foot.[10] I shall give the gentlemen an example in German of how this learned man wanted the caesura to be placed (though I do not know his position in regard to rhyme). For example, I might translate the beginning of *Plutus* this way:

> Ihr lieben Götter! haben wir nicht tausend Noth
> Wenn unsre Herren unverständge Narren sind.
> Denn giebt man ihnen tausendmal den besten Rath;
> Wenn sie sich einmal anders was in Kopf gesetzt:
> So büßt der Diener seines Herren Thorheit mit.[11]

If I may trust my ears, at least the sound of the unrhymed verses would be smoother this way because the lines are varied. The caesura endings are all feminine, and the end rhymes, masculine. The second half-verse, however, would have a totally different sound from the first. Finally, we would give our iambs a number of copulas, which up to now would either have had to be omitted or inserted only with considerable trouble. But I doubt that our ears, now accustomed to rhyme, can become accustomed to anything else.

I see very well that, in discussing this matter, I have strayed a little from my subject. But these things have such a direct

---

[9] "What a grievous thing it is, O Earth and gods [to be the slave of a foolish master]." The lines are spoken by Cario, slave of Cremylus, in Aristophanes' *Plutus*.

[10] In the twelfth line of Aristophanes' *Plutus*, μελαγχολῶντ' ἀπέπεμψέ μου τὸν δεσπότην ("He has sent my master off so moody-mad"—spoken by Cario), the caesura falls after μελαγχολῶντ'.

[11] In the English translation by B. B. Rogers, these lines are rendered:
> How hard it is, O Zeus and all ye gods,
> To be the slave of a demented master!
> For though the servant give the best advice,
> Yet if his owner otherwise decide,
> The servant needs must share the ill results.

—Aristophanes, *Plutus* 1–5, "Loeb Classical Library," No. 180 (London: Heinemann, 1927), III, 365.

connection to what I have been treating that my digression will surely be pardoned. And I shall return to my purpose.

If the question concerns the kind of meter that should be used in comedy or in drama generally, I allow that one should not choose the kind that violates our aims by striking a pathetic tone or one that has such a harmonious, almost singing, tone that it prevents the words from being spoken in the casual manner required for preserving the similarity to ordinary speech. In my estimation, this is what is meant when one says that the meter of comedy demands something that is like prose. It explains Aristotle's statement that iambic verse is chosen for comedies and tragedies because sometimes—and more often than with other verse forms—we tend to speak it more naturally and without thinking.[12] This is a rather definite indication that such verses are fully compatible with a natural manner of speaking, for in everyday life we do not generally, let us say, declaim; and there is nothing declamatory about the verses themselves.

The gentlemen have conceded this in regard to the verse of Greek and Latin comedies. It is my task to show that it is no less true of our German rhymed iambic verse. In this connection, they have proudly cited a Latin verse with six elisions as proof that it was impossible to have distinguished the verse lines in Roman comedy. If caprice rather than euphony inspired the laws of meter, I should like to believe that there was a time when one wrote verses that were no verses. But we

[12] In the *Rhetoric* (III.1, 1404a30–35), Aristotle points out the absurdity of the prose writer's imitating poetic diction when the poets themselves approach a style close to that of ordinary speech: "Just as iambics were adopted instead of tetrameter, because they are the most proselike of all metres, so tragedy has given up all those words, not used in ordinary talk, which decorated the early drama and are still used by the writers of hexameter poems. It is therefore ridiculous to imitate a poetical manner which the poets themselves have dropped." And in the *Poetics* (22, 1459a11–14), he says that "in iambic verse, which models itself as far as possible on the spoken language, only those kinds of words are in place which are allowable also in any oration, i.e., the ordinary word, the metaphor, and the ornamental equivalent."

cannot attribute such an empty notion to any people. The elisions they cite do not prove any such thing! It is impossible, they say, for all these syllables to have been swallowed if what was being said was to have been understood. And if the syllables were not swallowed, then one did not hear that it was verse. I ask them whether they concede that the Italians have verse and, what is more, of the kind that can be heard as such. I should hope that they do not deny this to a nation noted for its fine musical ear. And yet, in verses made to be spoken and permitting the highest degree of euphony, the Italians often do not hesitate, not merely to elide the vowels that the Romans syncopated, but even to elide as many as happen to occur successively into one syllable—something the Romans did not do. And they do this even if it means eliding a word consisting of one vowel with the last syllable of the preceding and the first of the succeeding word, thus making one syllable out of three.

I shall give them an example of five-foot iambs taken from a sonnet, a kind of poem certainly requiring no verses, which, according to their rule, we ought not to hear.

> Che se in fiumi converso alte, arenose
> Corna in alta e superbo urta e minaccia.[13]

In the first, we have three, in the second, four elisions. I have not wanted to take the trouble to locate them in any other way than to have them readily catch my eye. And, if they must grant me that four elisions do not render a five-foot verse line unrecognizable,

> Gli orecchi ho in Cielo e gli occhi in paradiso,[14]

then the same will be true of six elisions in a six-foot line.

[13] These lines, as well as Schlegel's other examples from Italian poetry, are taken from the 1706 (first) edition of Lodovico Antonio Muratori's anthology *Della perfetta poesia italiana*, IV, 226. The lines quoted, "that if, turned into rivers, [it] raises high, sandy branches and proudly strikes and threatens," are from a sonnet to the ocean (*gran padre delle cose—* "great father of things") by Antonio Vaccari. The missing subject, i.e., "it" in the translation, thus refers to the ocean.

[14] *Ibid.*, p. 390. "My ears I have in heaven, and my eyes, in paradise."

Likewise, if they want an example in which three syllables come together:

> Quanto é il suo Bello in te piu bello e vivo.[15]

If we take the example,

> Piangi o Rosa e tu sospiri,
> O Giacinto! Ahi duolo Ahi morte,[16]

it should strike them immediately that the first verse is a four-foot trochaic line. Thus they see that there are verses that people without correct pronunciation do not hear, whereas someone born in a language can hear them quite clearly as verses. The Italians, so far as I can judge from their singing, do not swallow these syllables because they are sung.

I admit that the iambic meter of the Romans, as it was used in the comedies, had less harmony than the meter of heroic poetry. The reason for this lay, however, not so much in the iambic meter itself as in the freedom one took with it. Horace used it in the odes, which he would not have done if one had not actually heard the verse in the iambs. But, if these verses had much less harmony than heroic verse, it still cannot be concluded that our verses are more harmonious than Roman verse—not even if we wanted to use as a comparison to Terence our present-day verse instead of that of older poets (that is, before our modern attentiveness made German verse so smooth). We certainly encounter unintentional iambic verse in our writings more often than the Romans in theirs. And one need be only a little lax in avoiding it for our writings to become full of such verses. If the iambic verse of our serious poetry takes on a tone that, of its own accord, as it were, causes a voice to sound pathetic and sublime, it does so after the caesura has become distinctly recognizable, after the nouns have been supplied with adjectives, and after the proper cadence

[15] *Ibid.*, p. 237. "How much her beauty is, in you, [even] more beautiful and lively."
[16] *Ibid.*, p. 452. "You cry, O rose, and you, O hyacinth, do sigh. Alas, pain! Alas, death!"

has been given. Pathos in our poetry is due, not to meter, but to the words and the tone we give them. But rhyme has absolutely nothing to do with the fact that the comic actor uses a different tone from that which he would use if he were speaking prose.

If the actor is clumsy and speaks his lines in a singsong, it should be attributed, not to rhyme or meter, but to bad habit or the fact that he believes that he is making the verses more euphonious. Altogether, one will find that it is difficult for people, whether they recite in verse or prose (which they read or speak from memory), to recite in a natural tone. But there is as little reason for so many speakers to recite verse unnaturally as to recite prose. If two rhymed verses can be spoken without either one forcing the actor to depart from his natural tone, then both together can be spoken naturally. If there is nothing in the one or the other to cause unnaturalness, I do not see how the relationship between the two should cause it. Imagine the two verses as being separate—in which case they would not ryhme—and have them spoken with complete naturalness, one a short time after the other. If both can be spoken quite naturally in separation, they can in unity as well.

I regret that we still have no published verse comedies and that I am therefore unable to offer the gentlemen an example for clarification. Meanwhile, I shall satisfy them by offering another illustration. Imagine that these lines, taken from a poet's praise of women, were being spoken in a theater:

Die Weiber kosten Geld. Ist das nicht eine Klage?
Was wiederholt ihr sie? Ihr mehrt ja nur die Plage.
Die Grillen helfen nichts. Die Noth wird nicht gestillt,
Sucht lieber Mittel vor, wie man den Beutel füllt.
Ist es nicht eure Pflicht, die Weiber zu ernähren?
Nur eure Trägheit sucht die Ordnung umzukehren.
Müßt ihr im Ehstand seyn? Ach, nein, es steht euch frey,
Daß ihr noch ledig bleibt. Doch denket ihr dabey,
Die Weiber sind doch gut: so müßt ihr euch bequemen,
Wenn ihr das Gute wollt, das Böse mitzunehmen.
Zu dem erwägt es selbst. Wer schließt wohl einen Stein,
Der nicht das mindste gilt, in sichre Kasten ein?

Was man umsonst erlangt, pflegt man für nichts zu schätzen,
Wir pflegen ja den Werth den Kosten gleich zu setzen;
So wird die Kostbarkeit der Weiber auch vermehrt,
Wenn Kost und Tracht und Schmuck den vollen Beutel leert.[17]

I hope that they will see nothing in these lines to force the actor to elevate his tone inopportunely or to resort to pathos. Thus, they see that one can write verses in our six-foot rhymed iambs perfectly suitable for comedy. And I have done what I set out to do. I have first refuted their principal objection; then I have disproved the others wherever I happened to encounter them; and I have shown that a verse comedy is superior to prose comedy and that part of the former's perfection is the very fact that it is written in verse. Finally, I have demonstrated that our kind of verse is eminently suitable for comedy. Having done this, I remain,

Yours truly,

S.

---

[17] Women cost money. Isn't that a vexing thing?
But why repeat it? You only increase the vexation.
Melancholy thoughts do not help; the trouble is not put aside.
Look rather for ways to fill your purse.
Is it not your duty to support women?
'Tis only your indolence that attempts to reverse the arrangement.
Must you be married? Why, no, you are at liberty
To stay single. But consider this, too:
Women are, after all, good; and so you must condescend
To take the bad along with the good.
Then, too, consider for yourselves: Who would lock a stone,
Which has no worth at all, inside a safety vault?
What one attains for nothing is not deemed worth a thing.
For we are wont to equate worth with cost;
And so the costliness of women is increased
When board and dress and finery empty a full purse.

—*Writings of the German Society*, Part III (1739). The author is unidentified. The periodical was a predecessor and, in its third and last volume, a competitor of Gottsched's *Critische Beiträge*.

Translator's Preface to Le Glorieux

A VERSE COMEDY IN FIVE ACTS
TRANSLATED FROM THE FRENCH
OF MONSIEUR NÉRICAULT DESTOUCHES
MEMBER OF THE FRENCH ACADEMY

I should do no favor to Destouches' reputation if I were to attempt to act as his herald here. My readers would justifiably be angry with me, believing that I considered them so indifferent to the fine arts as to know nothing of the achievements of a man capable of attracting world attention in an area of humor in which a Molière was his predecessor. Destouches himself felt the difficulty of attaining prominence after Molière. In his preface to *Le Glorieux*, he says:

In my plays, I can flatter myself with no other honor than that there appears to be a kind of originality in my plays, although it would appear that, after the incomparable Molière's endeavors, the only possible art of giving pleasure is to follow in his footsteps. And, yet, what temerity to attempt to imitate a model that the wisest and most judicious writers have always considered inimitable! Molière attained such heights that we must despair of rivaling him. Indeed, we must consider it extraordinary good fortune if, in the eyes of his readers and by having recourse to innovation, we manage to write tolerably well. In my dramatic works, my ambition went no further than this, and, no doubt, I owe the favorable reception given my plays to this necessary prudence.[1]

[1] "Toute la gloire dont je puisse me flatter, c'est d'avoir pris un ton qui a paru nouveau, quoiqu'après l'incomparable Molière il semblât qu'il n'y eût point d'autre secret de plaire que celui de marcher sur les traces. Mais quelle témérité de vouloir suivre un modèle que les auteurs les plus sages et les plus judicieux ont toujours regardé comme inimitable! Il ne nous a laissé que le désespoir de l'égaler. Trop heureux si, par quelque route nouvelle, nous pouvons nous rendre supportables après lui! C'est à quoi

Such is the modest way in which Destouches writes, and to this modesty he owes the fact that he created such masterpieces. Modesty makes great men charming. Yet, this is not its sole virtue; it even helps men become great.

My critical judgment could not be more presumptuous than if I wanted to determine the value and rating of his comedies and to judge which of his plays deserved first position. So I content myself with saying that Voltaire and the Abbé Prevost cite *Le Glorieux* before all other comedies by Destouches and that it is one of those pieces that has been taken up with greatest applause by witty and loathsome Paris.[2] Destouches (also from modesty) attributes the good reception of his play to the skill of the actors who performed it, and he can hardly praise them enough.

Because I had decided to translate a comedy, it was primarily this general approval that induced me to attempt *Le Glorieux*, and the quarrel between two good Leipzig friends concerning verse comedy inclined me to undertake the translation of such a play.[3]

One must not, for that reason, assume that I have openly taken sides. For, choose as I might, my judgment would appear only too partisan. If I sided with verse comedy, it would seem that I wanted to give my work a value surreptitiously; but, if I embraced the party that rejects verse comedy, it would seem

---

je me suis borné dans mes ouvrages dramatiques, et c'est sans doute à cette précaution essentielle que de dois l'accueil favorable qu'ils ont reçu" —Destouches' "Preface" to the play, in *Théâtre de Destouches*, ed. Louis Moland (Paris, 1878), p. 123.

[2] Voltaire and the Abbé Prevost: In his *Catalogue de la plupart des écrivains français*, Voltaire writes, "Sa comédie du *Glorieux* est son meilleur ouvrage, et probablement restera au théâtre" ("His comedy *Le Glorieux* is his best work and will probably remain in the theater."— *Œuvres complètes de Voltaire* [Paris, 1826], 25, 119). No theatrical criticism is published in the Abbé Prevost's collected works. However, the periodical *Le Pour et Contre*, published by Prevost from 1733 to 1740, contains reviews of principal contemporary works, and it is probable that Destouches' play was so praised in this periodical.

[3] See Introduction, p. xxii.

that I was trying to take revenge on the form for the trouble and difficulties it caused me. Indeed, if I were called on to give my true feelings, I doubt that I would be able to because I simply do not know whether I hold an opinion. Not long ago, I was still an adherent of one side, but most people begin by knowing and only afterward learn to doubt. And so the reasons of the opposing side are neither so weak as to keep me from wavering nor so strong as to convince me.

I now believe that if there is any adducible reason to support verse comedy it is not one that proves more than it should and applies to all the arts that imitate nature. I am referring, namely, to the reason offered against opera—and, perhaps, no more felicitously than against verse comedy. As it has been said of opera that it is unnatural for heroes to sing of their deeds, rage, and compassion, so has it been said of verse comedy that it is unnatural for ordinary people to express their decisions and ideas in rhyme. But, if it is unnatural for poetry to imitate the actions of bourgeois life in verse and the emotions of heroes in verse and music simultaneously, then it is likewise unnatural for sculpture to imitate living bodies by means of inanimate ones or, for example, black horses by white marble (which is smooth and hairless) or a horse's mane, which consists of an infinite number of little parts, by a piece of marble hewn to resemble the surface of a mane. And it is unnatural for painting to represent solid bodies by means of surfaces or for copper engraving to render polychromatic objects by means of monochromatic surfaces. Prose and verse do not differ as much as solid bodies and planes do; at least the difference between the first two is no greater than between the last two.

If one rejects rhyme and meter in comedy and sung tones in opera because this property of the imitations conflicts with a quality inherent in and inseparable from the thing imitated (which is to say that, if the speech of ordinary men is never measured or rhymed and the threats of kings never sung), then one will have to damn all the aforementioned arts. The property of a carved figure, namely, the fact that it is of wood, is necessarily at variance with the characteristic of a living figure made of flesh. Between the essential characteristics of a living tree (it is a body, its trunk can be embraced, and its leaves touched on both sides) and the essential characteristics of a painted tree (it occupies no solid space, its trunk cannot be encompassed nor its leaves touched on both sides)—between these characteristics, there exists an open contradiction.

Therefore, those who attack verse comedy on the grounds that it is too difficult or downright impossible to impose meter on dialogue without rendering it unnatural and that the lesser charm imparted by meter to a work must give way to the greater one that allows a comedy natural dialogue—those who do this know better the nature of poetry. The condemnation or vindication of verse comedy depends on the proof or refutation of these grounds. That verse comedy is not impossible for the French and that naturalness of dialogue does not suffer in this form is actively proven by Molière, Destouches, Regnard, author of the *Modevorurtheil*, etc.;[4] Therefore, the quarrel should be restricted to German verse comedy. We cannot consider the quarrel settled and conclude that, because French meter does not make dialogue sound unnatural, the same would hold true for German meter. German prosody is a far sterner tyrant than is French prosody. We have long and short syllables, and our meter demands the proper variation of the two. This is especially true of comedies, the nature of which requires the most regular verse. The French do not have long and short syllables, and, consequently, their meter does not have such a requirement.

Having philosophized more than I should, it is time to beg my reader's pardon for this loquacity. Perhaps he believes that I wanted only to strengthen my views secretly, since I have explained above why I do not hold any opinion on these matters at the moment. Those who are convinced of the difficulties of verse comedy and, therefore, expect nothing good of my trans-

[4] The author of the *Modevorurtheil* or, in the original, *Le Préjugé à la mode*, is Nivelle de la Chaussée (1692–1754), well-known dramatist and member of the Academy.

lation can be satisfied to a degree by the quality of the original, which has beauties to sacrifice.

Does my translation, then, dare go forth into the world? And can it be well received, since translators are considered near-traitors to their country and enemies of German fame? As soon as one sees a new publication, one says, "It isn't by chance another translation, is it?" I do not know whether these stern critics ask whether it is a good German original, but I do know that, before they deem it presentable to the Germans, they ask whether it is a German original. We Germans have long been accustomed to congratulating ourselves on the perfection of our poetry and the merits of our wit. One need only refer to the poets' prefaces that have been appearing for several centuries in Germany to see how most of them prove in great detail that German language and poetry have now attained their peak. Their successors have usually remarked that their forebears scarcely reached the first step. They recognized this fact. But, gradually and just as unfortunately as their predecessors, they, too, fell into the habit of considering the peak of the German Parnassus conquered. Never have our congratulations on the high position we hold been more frequent or ardent than in recent years. And who would assure us that we can now do without the foreigners—who, until now, have had to lead us by the hand—because we are now strong enough to walk alone? Who would assure us that translations are presently not as useful as they were twenty and more years ago? I may at least be permitted to doubt our greatness, because our patriotism can otherwise easily blind us in this regard.

Leipzig
August 1, 1745